CAIRNS CASTLE.
(Walter G. Grieve, R.S.A.)

PENTLAND DAYS
& COUNTRY WAYS

A WALKER'S WALLET

BY

WILL GRANT

AUTHOR OF
"THE CALL OF THE PENTLANDS"

WITH THIRTY ILLUSTRATIONS
FROM PHOTOGRAPHS AND
A FRONTISPIECE IN COLOUR

THOMAS NELSON AND SONS, Ltd.
LONDON, EDINBURGH, NEW YORK
TORONTO, AND PARIS

TO

LOVERS OF THE

HILLS OF HOME

THE WIDE WORLD

O'ER

CONTENTS

Contents

LIST OF ILLUSTRATIONS

PENTLAND DAYS

INTRODUCTION

THE Pentland countryside is rich in the glamour and romance of literary, historical, and antiquarian lore ; rich also in the stories of her hill folk and their ancient arts and crafts—farmers and shepherds, keepers and carriers, poachers and drovers, weavers and cobblers and whimsical lairds. And as we take our way among the hills and the country places, over drove roads and moorland tracks, and by burns and streams, we have conversation with rare personalities who spend their days and win their livelihood among the open spaces, and we find how much there is of pleasure and delight in the local legends, tales, and stories. So here is a Walker's Wallet of Pentland Days and Country Ways—walking adventures, hillside reveries and inspirations, mysteries, strange discoveries and knightly romance, with curious legends and sporting stories, gathered from the hill folks themselves and from chroniclers of long ago.

Variety of impressions and the gift of being able to see the humorous side of things add much to the spice of life. What, then, more pleasant than the recollection in tranquillity of days upon the hills—the freshness and sweetness of morning and evening scents and sounds, the magic sunshine and the misty rain, the blue skies and the heaven-reflecting waters, the green hillsides and the purple pine woods? Then there are the talks in Lowden Doric we have enjoyed at farm steadings and cottage doors as we lingered on the road, and stories told in the inn as we rested at the close of day.

As in thought we tramp the hills again, may we feel the call of the hills, smell the tang of the heather and the bracken, hear the cry of the whaups and peewits in the glen and uplands, and taste anew the Pentland wine, mellow, moorland-scented, and satisfying ; may there blow in upon us and around us an aroma of the Hills of Home, and all that they stand for, laden with fragrant memories—joys of Pentland Days and Country Ways, and jolly tales from the hills !

Most of the chapters of this book have appeared in various journals and magazines—*The Scotsman, The Weekly Scotsman, The Edinburgh Evening Dispatch, The Edinburgh Evening News, The S.M.T. Magazine,* and *The Scots Magazine.* These, together with new matter, are now published in their present form in the hope that the Wallet may be found as companionable as the friendly hills themselves. My grateful thanks are due to Mr. J. Laurence Tweedie for his painstaking care in securing the photographic illustrations, and for the artistic quality of his work.

WILL GRANT.

Chapter I

THE CALL OF THE HILLS

RICHARD JEFFERIES said there were two periods in the year when the country, with its far spaces, its hills and mystic sounds, awoke in him the migratory impulse. Every year from boyhood he felt it in the month of March, and often so powerfully as to be quite unable to resist it. " Go I must," he writes, " and go I do somewhere."

So it is with the Walker, the Nature lover. That springtime call is not to be denied. It is a hunger of the spirit, and he knows that it can be satisfied, for out beyond the city boundaries the hills are calling, the curlews and lapwings are crying, and down the cool, exhilarating wind comes the scent of heather-burning, and the flavour of wet moorlands kissed by the sun. With each recurring spring he recalls with a certain wistfulness the Wise Man's Canticle, for he knows it to be true—" Rise up, my love, my fair one, and come away. For, lo, the winter is past, the rain is over and gone ; the flowers appear on the earth ; the time of the singing of birds is come."

And so we set off for the old familiar places among the hills, hoping to be caught up again by the spirit of Nature that brings joy and peace. " The sweet voices of Nature," said Coleridge, " are always full of love and joyance."

The healing influences come flooding in upon us as we open mind and heart to the full impression of the clean, fresh winds of heaven, the great wide spaces above wherein white galleons proudly sail, the song in the trees, the discovery of nests among the grasses ; and we seek out the solitary places, visit the high tops, the cleughs and the lochans.   We explore the watercourses, make friends with the streams and the paths ; we study the personality of the hills, and ponder deeply upon the hill silence.   The eerie sough in the sound of these memory-haunted names—the Windy Gowl, the Cauld-staneslap, the Garval Syke—sends us out upon fresh adventure, and we feel that the Cairns, far Craigengar, and Byrehope Mount are calling us no less than the Kips, Scald Law, and Carnethy.

For quiet interest and companionship there is much to be said for the little stream, the " burn," for it has character, and a voice of its own that tells in varied tones the secrets of the high hills and the corries.   By turns it talks and chatters, is loud and boisterous, and croons a lullaby, and its confiding frankness wins the heart. It enlivens the whole landscape, and draws us to its banks ; it bids us follow to its loneliest heights where beauty and wonder reign supreme in quiet simplicity. The more intimate our companionship the stronger becomes our love for the stream that charms us.   So Naaman thought long ago : " Are not Abana and Pharpar, rivers of Damascus, better than all the waters of Israel ? "

In its course it plays like a child, yet with skilled and loving artistry it carves the grassy borders and the golden sands, flushing the pools under heather and bush, and keeping the reeds and the tall flowers nodding as it flows ; then in laughter pouring over shelving rocks, to become a shining mirror for Nature to view her charms afresh. So does Nature work her enchantments with music and with colour.

At evening, birds call us to listen to the fairy melody of the stream—richer and softer now, for it is attuned to the hush of the gloaming hour, and its secret message we fain would learn to understand. "There is no music like a little river's," said R. L. S. ; "it quietens a man down like saying his prayers."

No walk arouses so much curiosity and expectancy as that over the unknown path that winds and twists over moorland and hill, by coppice and ferny brake, by fence and farm and standing cattle, by woods of purple mist and mossy turf, scented of wood violets and soft as cony wool.

It is a glamourous quest that appeals to us all, taking us to quiet places, where startled moorcock and pheasant may rise and thrushes flute their warning notes ; to a spring or river bank, where timid creatures of fur and feather come to drink at dawn and dusk ; a ford where stepping-stones reveal the pathway of keepers, fishers, shepherds. Doubtless the path was first made by animals in daily search of food and water and rest, and was followed by man the hunter and the colonizer, and so on through the centuries down to the present time when Nature's children use it still. The wayfarer values it as a legacy from the past. In such paths he finds peace and serenity. For some of us the silent winding sunlit path will for ever remain a pathway of romance. What joys will it bring ? What delight of anticipation ? Whither will it wander ? What vistas will it open when we round the bend—what new peaks and valleys and streams ? We speculate, we dream, we hasten our steps, we breast the incline and stand upon the eminence, surprising the deer, the wild duck, or the heron ; anticipation becomes reality ; and when the day's adventure closes, memory stores it all away —its broad impressions, its minute details—for happy hours of quiet thinking, for in that sunny land those hill paths have immortal life.

Hills have personality. We either like a certain hill, or we dislike it, at the first impression of its individuality. If hills are our friends they are also our benefactors, for they bring back to us our youth by their changelessness, and despite all changes in ourselves we are renewed with the same feelings as of yore. Strange influences thrill the soul, and the keen desire to renew the experience whenever opportunity offers is evidence of their real companionship. He who has enjoyed a long day's tramp over the hills knows what that means.

What we prize most in human friendship—constancy and comfort—we find in our friends the hills. They bring us back to our real selves ; they restore to us a true balance and perspective of life. There is a correspondence between the personality of the hills and our own personality, but it is not always easy to interpret —they are so great in the vast scheme of Nature, so mysterious, representing an everlasting natural order, and providing us with countless symbols of the supernatural, which imagination delights to pursue.

It was Coleridge who said that it has been the music of gentle and pious minds in all ages, and it is the poetry of all human life, to read the book of Nature in a figurative sense, and to find therein symbols of the spiritual world. Perhaps this is one reason why the hills are for ever calling us, giving to us as we tramp along not only physical recreation and mental quickening, but also renewal of æsthetic pleasure and spiritual exaltation, and a desire for the fuller experience and mellowed wisdom that comes with the passing of the years.

There is something strange and wonderful about the silence of the hills. Always the hills seem to intensify the silence, no matter when or where it may be experienced—in the hush of a summer dawn before sunrise, in the late afternoon of a winter day amidst the snow-capped peaks, in the gloaming of an autumn night when the rosy sun sends good-night kisses across the sky, or in summer days when " all the air a solemn stillness holds." Always they seem to shed an influence which assures us that we are not alone, that we are one with the quiet hills, one with Nature.

For an instant the silence grips the heart, eclipses time and space, stirs the emotions and the intellect ; it is the moment of imaginative insight, when the spirit is one with the " speaking " silence. But what is learned in that brief flash of illumination may never find expression. We too are silent ; it is the silence that comes with the consciousness of a great experience. But who has not felt that the hill silence leaves impressions deep as scars upon the memory, rich in portent for the soul's adventure and content ? No Walker who is a lover of the hills could be a materialist, or lightly esteem the reality of such emotions.

The real Walker and Nature lover knows the woods

and the waters where spring evenings bear the spell of an enchantment—echo-haunted out-of-way places, where the birds are shouting with the ecstasy of love ; and as springtime merges into summer he views the dawn— the symbol of eternal youth—in which the scene reaches a climax of surpassing loveliness that thrills us through and through. The sky is flooded with light ; it pours out to the farthest reach in wave upon wave, ranging from rosy pink to pearly whiteness, and the music is provided by the symphony of larks high above us, raining down their song upon the dewy earth.

He has his familiar viewpoints that he visits to see the fading of the light of day, places to remember, hallowed by memories of this Sacrament of Hope. There are also other points where he has watched the lights appear in lonely cottages and farm dwellings in the gloaming of November nights. And who that has stood upon the heights of Howden Glen or Allermuir in the Pentlands on a night of stars, and gazed upon the illuminated city, guarded by the Lion, the Rock, and the Sea, but has had his imagination stirred, his vision cleansed, his perspective enlarged, and his love for " Auld Reekie " heightened and deepened ?

There is much to be said for the walk that is enjoyed with some kindred spirit, who knows when to talk and when to keep silence, but there are times when the Walker wants to be alone. Nature does not reveal herself to all, nor to any all at once ; her companionship is of slow growth ; it is to the solitary and undistracted spirit that she opens her great heart.

When starting upon your walk, relax both mind and muscle. Walk easily, slowly, steadily. Shut everything out of your mind. Let Nature's alchemy trans-

THE ROAD TO THE HILLS.

form you wholly before you do anything else. It may take half an hour, it may take three hours, but do not talk, except it be of some nature note or striking view that has attracted your attention, until the re-creating work has had a good start. Nature has far too much to say to permit either serious discussion or idle talk. Be quiet and still, until on through the day come fresh moods and new experiences, a satisfaction and contentment never known before, and finally the day passes to rest in the peace of eventide. Oh, the tenderness, the graciousness of Nature's benediction at such times! And we link those times with the places where we have known them, where strange things have happened that left their impression deep upon the soul. In the temple of the hills we are in touch with things eternal. That is the secret of the hillman's love and his full surrender to the Call of the Hills.

Chapter II

WESTWARDS

AUTUMN days upon the hills—how good they are, with their fresh winds and open sunny skies! They mark the beginning of the winter walking season for the hill enthusiast. The clear cool air with a touch of frost, the magic autumn colourings, and all the joys of exercise bring once more a longing for the hills and the far horizons; the old tramping suit and greased boots are brought out again, and knapsack on back and cromak in hand the hillman wanders forth.

We were westward bound; the open spaces beyond the Cauldstaneslap were calling; and in the early morning we faced the freshening breeze blowing straight from Tinto's Tap, breasting many an upland slope and heathery moorland as the day went on, till the evening shadows gathered round us on the heights above Dunsyre.

As we set out upon the long straight road from Balerno that passes Johnsburn and Butelandhill, there is a sound of running water, a rustling of leaves, and the chattering of many a runnel by the field's edge. It is good to have a road like this upon which to start a day's walk. It is not too hard, exercise of muscle is gradual, it is free from traffic, the eye finds rest on every side, and unconsciously we gain that receptive mood that means renewal of mind and body.

Kaimes Hill on our right is rapidly being eaten up by the roadmakers, and now there is a great gash in its side. In the morning sunshine the bare brown rock contrasts with the green hillside and the white harvest fields below. Mid-October has come and gone, but still there are sheaves in the open fields, and the warm sunshine is as welcome to the farmer as it is to the Walker. It brings joy to the hearts of all, illumines the myriad colours in every place, and makes the glory of the perfect autumn day. Here are hawthorns with clusters of berries flaming red, and leaves of green and yellow and purple; over the lea lies the whitewashed homestead—blue and red and gold are the mellow lichened roofs, and store of golden grain is stacked within the grey-ringed yard. Colours everywhere! How the sunshine of the autumn days makes vivid to eye and imagination the glorious wealth of variety and contrast of Nature's bounteous store.

Over the Temple Hill we go. Now we are making for the Cairn Hills, and soon we shall be inhaling deep draughts of Pentland wine from the topmost heights. At this season of soft, mellow light the hills do not appear to be rejoicing as they do in the dancing light of spring and summer days; rather do they impress us with their quiet stolidity, their strength and resignation —perhaps that is the secret of their appeal to the winter Walker. There is still a brightness and a gladness in the moorland, although it is becoming more silent, the lemon-coloured grass is fading to whiteness or glowing to russet, and the tang of the sun-kissed moistures revives past memories. The wind rises and falls, and there is " the sound of a going " in the tops of the fir trees. Thoughts come quick and sharp, vision becomes widened as the prospect of the free horizon opens out. The nibbling sheep look up and gaze in wonder ; we also wonder at the marvellous transforming power of this hill air, for the body has lost its weight, brain and muscle respond without labour or effort, senses are quickened, sympathies are enlarged.

We pause to examine the dry-stane dyke that crosses the Slap, for never did it look so beautiful as it does to-day. Colours innumerable are here among the clean dry stones—stones of every hue are reflecting the light, some with facets of quartz and mica glisten and shine like stars in the firmament on a frosty night, others are mottled in lichen growths of ebony, red, and golden green, and around the base of this dry-built wall ferns and mosses, heather and blaeberry grow and flourish.

The bare moorland around the West Cairn also has its interest ; it is the free domain of the blue mountain hare, now in the first stage of changing colour. One of them watches me as I sit upon a jutting ledge covering a fox's den, where I had disturbed him at his toilet. Next comes a confiding spider, and I find that he appears to enjoy bread and jam ; then two hoodie crows begin to quarrel on the hilltop above me—perhaps over the lifeless wild duck I had passed among the heather half an hour ago.

Around the outcrop of giant rocks that stand out so solemnly upon the remote hillside overlooking the Wolf Craigs we come to the greatest treasure of all the glory of this autumn day—the colours of the marshy moor-land mosses, velvety, soft, and delicate—tender shades

DUNSYRE HILL FROM GARVALD.

of green and orange and crimson, now in separate patches, now blended in mosaic patterns.

The secret places of the westland moors become more difficult as we travel, for they contain stretches of sphagnum retaining full measure of the summer's rain. Soon the daylight begins to fade, the sunshine leaves us, and it seems as if it were the hour "when summer gathers up her robes of glory, and like a dream of beauty glides away." A greyness settles over the hills. Where are now the joyous notes of the glowing colour symphony and all the feast of imaginings that the blue skies flecked with fleecy clouds had brought? How varied are the moods of an autumn day!

The wind has fallen. There is a stillness and a silence in the wide strath where the hills fill every horizon. Then a strange thing happens. Is it a grouse that has been wounded or winged that comes flopping towards us through the tussocky grass? We stand still, the bird makes several forward movements, then lies quiet. Immediately a sharp brown head shoots up; it is not the head of a grouse, but that of a weasel, which is apparently endeavouring to carry off the bird. He made no sound, but gazed at us fixedly for a second, then slunk off. On coming forward we found that most of the "innards" of the bird were gone, although the feathers of wing and back were intact. Doubtless the weasel was taking the bird home for the young ones. He had carried it some fifty yards, for at that distance many feathers were found where the tragedy had taken place.

It was now time for us to consider where our destination was to be, for so long as we kept tramping westwards we little cared whether it was Carnwath, Dunsyre, or Dolphinton, but the greyness of late afternoon was gathering, and we quickened our pace. Far on the right appears the clump of trees that caps the bare hill near where the Auchengray and Harburn rights-of-way join at the Garval Syke, and we bear to the left in order to strike the Catstone Hill. It has been steady going for the last few miles through marshy moorland and tufted grass, into which at certain places it was easy to thrust one's cromak up to the neck, but there is higher and harder ground at hand where the going is good, keeping the Medwin Water on our right and crossing the Ravens' Cleuch between the Millstone Rig and Fadden Hill. This cleuch is as interesting to explore as the deep winding valley of the Medwin; and the screes upon the hillside show the fierce attrition of the wintry storms that beat upon this lonely place. It is, however, a merry little amber-coloured burn that flows from the sequestered watershed, for it chatters over all its rock-bound course and golden gravel pools till it joins the Medwin Water.

As we crossed the top of Catstone Hill the view to the westwards was sombre and awe-inspiring—over the valley of Dunsyre and among the wavy hollows around the Covenanter's Grave lay an amethystine haze like the bloom upon a ripened peach or plum, while the White Hill, the Black Mount, and the rock above Dunsyre stood out like sentinels guarding the Roman Way that led through the pass to Cleghorn.

In the gathering gloom a silence brooded over the eerie moorland, yet we were sure we heard fairy voices and "horns of elfland faintly blowing" as we passed the fir wood, into which the white scuts of conies had flashed a moment ago. And our destination? Was it

to be the shepherd's cottage or the farmer's house where
we were to find rest and refreshing? Hill-walkers and
tramps know where the kind hearts dwell, and there are
many among the hill folks around the Hills of Home.

One good woman, whose picturesque little cottage lies
under the shelter of the western hills, often narrates to
me the stories of her visitors of the tramp fraternity,
who call at regular intervals. " Ma'm," said one the
other day, " the last time I was here ye gied me a grand
plate o' broth." " And when was that ? " she queried,
knowing that he could tell to a day when last he called.
" Just a year come next Seturday." " Well, come awa'
in, and ye'll get another plate o' broth." Then out
comes the story of his wanderings, and she listens to it
all like a mother, for she has an understanding heart,
and interjecting words of wisdom here and there she
soon gains their confidence. The way to their hearts
is easy for her, and after warming them and feeding
them, off they go again, blessing her as they depart,
while she muses as the round shoulders and the green
coat disappear at the bend of the road—" Puir fella,
he had been something better, but—ay, there's aye
some reason at the bottom o' it a', every time," but she
never judges. Hers is a charity that forgives all.

But it is not alone the tramps that come to her door.
On one occasion a bare-headed man came in the darkening, and asked if he could have a cup of tea as he had
been tramping the hills all day, and had heard of her
hospitable cottage from a shepherd on the heights.
" I'm a traveller," he said, as she shouldered him into
the kitchen. " You'll be wondering who and what I
am," he continued. " Ay, a traiveller, are ye ? " she
replied ; " an' what for ? Is it groceries or drapery or

what ? " " No, no," he answered, " guess again ; what do you think I look like ? " " Well, maybe you'll be a photographer, or something like that ? " " No," he replied very humbly, " I'm a minister, a parish minister, and there's nothing does me so much good as a day on the hills." " Ay, whaur's yer kirk, then ? " she inquired anxiously, and so they came to know each other. " A fine crack we had, and losh ! I was sorry when it was time for him to be off, we had sae mony things in common ! "

It was dark as we walked into the farmyard, but we must first poke our heads into the byre, for the purring sound of milk falling into a pail is music in the townsman's ear. Then we rapped on the door, and the ruddy glow of the firelight that greeted us when the master himself opened to us made our welcome doubly joyful. Few places around the hills are more cosy than a farmer's ingle after a day's tramp.

Soon, too soon, we had to set out again, for there were still a couple of miles through field and woodland for us to cover before we could reach the Biggar highway, and the night was dark ; so dark that the farmer himself must accompany us. His horny hand was hard, but it was gentle, and he guided us as a father would his children through the darkness. And as we rested on the homeward journey our thoughts were of the sweetness and simplicity to which the day had brought us, and of the quiet peace that filled the heart, which would hold us fast till the Call of the Hills should once more take possession of us, and send us forth again in the old spirit of adventure—Westwards—across the Pentlands.

Chapter III

THE CAULDSTANESLAP: OLD TIME FORAYS

THE Cauldstaneslap is the gap or pass between the East and West Cairn Hills that dominate the western end of the Pentland range. It is well known to all Hill-walkers because of its situation upon an old right-of-way through the hills linking the Lang Whang with Linton Roderick on the Lyne.

Lord Sands once propounded the question, " How did rights-of-way begin ? " and answered it by saying, " Few of them could be primeval paths older than private property in land, and express grants of right-of-way must have been exceedingly rare. . . . All that was required to prove a right-of-way was that the road should have been used by the public as of right for forty years"; and Mr. H. P. Macmillan (Lord Macmillan) has written : " The origin of many of the Scottish rights-of-way is a matter of ancient history. Some of the most famous trace their existence back to the times when their rough tracks served as the only means of passage from one part of the country to another, and many of them are old drove roads."

The Cauldstaneslap right-of-way is one of the most noted of these old drove roads, and was in use for over four hundred years—a road over which cattle were driven from Scotland to England, a road that earned for itself the opprobrious title " The Thieves' Road."

It was a far cry from Lochaber and the Highlands to the English markets, but it was by this road that the drover came south, by Stirling and Falkirk, and through the Slap, on to Linton, Newlands, Lyne, and Stobo, over Scrape and Dollar Law, into Tweeddale and across the Cheviots, driving large herds of black cattle for hundreds of miles through wild and mountainous country, in fair weather and in foul, for weeks and months at a time, entailing upon the drover a life of strenuous toil, endurance, and responsibility.   There was good reason why the kilted Highlander carried a skean dhu, and why he slept in the open, night after night, with his charges. Every journey was an adventure ; danger lurked in every mile of it.   Yet it was the life he loved ; he was a stranger to fear, claimed freedom as a birthright, and beguiled the miles whistling a pibroch or singing a Highland song, as with his cudgel he urged forward the laggards of the herd.

He loved the life of motion, and the constant variety of the day's march, the intercourse with farmers, traders, and graziers, and the occasional merrymakings with cronies from the Highlands and drovers from Eskdale and Liddesdale.   He was proud of the confidence placed in him not only as being guardian of the herd, but responsible for its disposal to the best advantage, and experience made him cannily astute in making bargains. His cattle were his sole concern.   He avoided the highways, which distressed the bullocks' feet, and the turnpike annoyed his freedom-loving spirit.   He knew the necessity of bringing his beasts to market in good condition and free from leg-weariness ; the green places where feeding was obtainable, and the resting-places where there was water, were as well known to him as the places where danger lurked. His wants were meagre— a few handfuls of oatmeal, some onions, and a ram's-horn of whisky. A strong, wild, unkempt figure of a man if you will, with weather-beaten face and shaggy beard, and a bonnet stuck on his tousy head, but reliable, and touchy to a fault upon any point of honour. He was a man who could be trusted. His black cattle were valuable, and after they were sold he returned with his pocket-book filled with bank notes or his sporran lined with gold ; and it was this that made the drover's life a dangerous one. Many an encounter took place in the Cauldstaneslap, when blood was spilt and sheep and cattle stolen. Not without reason was it called " The Thieves' Road "—a road frequented by Border raiders and rievers, robbers and moss-troopers, and it was necessary that the drover should have a stout heart as well as a strong arm, and know how to use a dirk.

The name Cauldstaneslap has an eerie sough in the sound of it, and it was an eerie place, whether in the black darkness of a winter night and the howling of the storm, when the cruel north wind was tearing through the Slap, or on a still night of fitful moonlight, and woe betide the drover and his herd that were resting there when upon the wings of the wind came the thudding of horses' hoofs and the jingling of spurs and bridles. There are records of such raids in the books of the Privy Council. At midnight on Hallowe'en in 1582 a whole stock of ewes and wethers was stolen by a band of Armstrongs and Liddells in the Slap ; a similar raid took place in 1598, when a band of Scott of Branxholm's men raided the cattle at Easter Colzium ; two years later, in broad daylight, one August day, at Harper-rig, eighty oxen and several horses were stolen and the shepherds butchered. The Warden of the Slap in Cairns Castle was powerless, and there was no redress—the raiders were off like the wind, and the cattle impounded in the Devil's Beef Tub. It was possible, however, to purchase immunity from the depredations of the moss-troopers by paying blackmail in the shape of a yearly tax.

When the drover had sold his cattle in the South, he often returned to Linton, and bought sheep which were driven over the Slap to the Highlands, there to be fattened and driven back again later. Linton was the chief market in Scotland from 1631 to 1856 for the famous Linton breed of black-faced, black-legged, horned, and coarse-wooled sheep that were a favourite purchase by the Highland graziers. And when it is remembered that, in addition to the droves of black cattle that came from the North, 30,000 sheep were sold in the two market days at Linton in June for many years in the eighteenth century, we obtain some idea of the amount of traffic that went over this old drove road through the Cauldstaneslap.

From deeds dating as far back as the fourteenth century we learn that this road across the hills was a highway—it was named " the high road of the Carns (Cairns) " ; and in a charter of an adjoining stretch of upland near Newlands, granted by the Abbot of New-battle and his convent in 1532, we read " the lands are sterile of grain and crops, and as regards cattle have been practically waste and useless for many years past owing to the invasions of Border thieves."

The records of the Privy Council tell not only the tales of Border raiders in the Cauldstaneslap, they also

MEDWIN WATER.

tell of those who were raided by the King's Dragoons in the days of Scotland's Solemn League and Covenant. At one Conventicle on the Cairn Hills in 1684, between two and three hundred men and women were present with " blunderbushes, swords, pistolls, and other murdering wapons," and seven days later they again met "to hear the Word" at the "Caldstaineslope or some other places thereabout"—the other places being no doubt the wild and rugged ravines around the source of the Medwin, at the Garval Syke, and under the shelter of the Wolf Craigs. Equally good hiding-places were found among the giant boulders that surround the circular cairn on the East Cairn Hill. In 1684 Lawson of Cairnmuir was summoned before the Privy Council for not " dispersing Conventicles," probably upon his own lands and in his own farm buildings.

The Cauldstaneslap was a royal route also, for did not the eighteen-year-old King James the Fourth set out from Linlithgow upon a horse which he purchased there and ride through the Slap on November 25, 1490 ? The laird of Cairnmuir, Sir Richard Lawson of Hieriggs, Lord Justice-Clerk (1488), and Lord Provost of Edinburgh (1492–1505), was one of his councillors during his minority ; and it was the beauty of Lawson's daughter that occasioned the fierce combat between Meldrum of the Binns and Sir Lewis Stirling in Leith Walk in 1516, the tragic details of which are contained in Grant's *Old and New Edinburgh*. There were Lawsons in Cairnmuir for three centuries from before the year 1500, noted for kind-hearted generosity and wise and faithful lairdship. The young king was a frequent visitor to Linton.

As we near the end of our walk over the undulating heathery moorland we come in view of Mendick Hill

and the well-kept Linton Golf Course, laid out on the
lands of Slipperfield in 1890, and so arrive at the site
of the old sheep markets that once presented such a
busy scene, and the famous old inn—the Bridgehouse,
or Brig'us—that stood on the romantic coach road to
Biggar, Moffat, and Dumfries, an inn much frequented
by travellers.   In 1715 it had " lately been repaired."
One of its proprietors, James Wedderspuine, is described
as " one of the Peeblesshire gentry implicated in the
murder of Rizzio."   Burns called twice at the inn, but
found the landlord Graham from home, whereupon he
wrote upon the window pane, " Honest Graham, aye
the same, never tae be fand at hame."

Two incidents of the time of Prince Charlie are associated with Cairnmuir and with the inn.   A company of
roving Highlanders are reported to have gone to the
house and demanded food, but " Lady Cairnmuir " was
equal to the occasion, for she asked them by whose leave
they dared to enter her room without uncovered heads.
Off came the white-cockaded bonnets at once, and the
hungry fellows were supplied with a hearty meal, but
they ill requited the good lady, for they carried off the
pony belonging to her youngest son, whom they met on
the way ; just as they had stolen the Glencorse minister's
horse when they failed to obtain an entrance to the
manse.

The wife of the Prince's secretary — Murray of
Broughton—infected with the plundering spirit of the
times, commandeered from the inn stables two horses
belonging to Charles Hope of Craigiehall, whose servant
was in the inn, and ordered him to deliver £1000 and
valuable jewels.   Murray himself came out from Edinburgh to escort the booty.

The last of the Bourbon kings, Charles X., is also reputed to have stayed at the inn while shooting over the Slipperfield moors early in the nineteenth century.

But the winding track in the Cauldstaneslap is a drove road no longer, the Linton markets with their noise and bustle have disappeared, and the old inn has been incorporated in Medwyn House. There are no robbers or raiders, smugglers or hunted men, in the Slap to-day. A stillness lies over the valley, and a sense of wild, sweet solitude characterizes the spot. All is peace save for the bleating of sheep and the wild birds' cry. The strong castle of Cairns, the old-time Sentinel of the Slap, with ruined tower and vaulted basement, dungeons and cellars, incrusted with the age of the centuries, has now become one with the silence of the hills. It stands dreaming by the waters of Harper-rig, embowered in leafy foliage, and sheltered by the West Cairn—a fitting relic in a charming landscape whose spirit is redolent not only of " winds austere and pure," but also of a peace that is satisfying and inexhaustible. We are glad that no modern highway has been made upon the ancient right-of-way, for hill-walkers are jealous guardians of the opportunity that the hills afford to participate in the tonic of sublime tranquillity that Nature offers to the hearts of those who love her. Nowhere is it more effective than among the hills around the Cauldstaneslap. Here surely the heart is filled with the peace of the solitudes, and the mind soothed with " tranquil restoration."

Chapter IV

WHERE THE LYNE FLOWS

PLEASANT days may be spent among the hills in tracing the courses of the rivers and waters, such as the North Esk, Medwin, West Water, Pollentarf, and Lyne, which all abound in surprises and unexpected places, providing a day's recreation of pure delight. Let us see where the Lyne flows, and follow its course.

Lyne is called a " water "—a term used in the south of Scotland to indicate a small river—larger than a burn, and midway between the English " rivulet " and " river." The term " burn," on the other hand, was once upon a time used for a water that was sufficient to drive a small water-wheel for light machinery. This water rises in the hilly landscape under the East Cairn Hill, a wild heathery moorland inhabited by moor birds, foxes, and conies, and the descendants of mountain hares that were first set free on the Pentlands in 1867–68. Wonder and awe are added to the scene by the mysterious " hilltop " cairn, while at the Roman Camp, where Lyne joins Tweed, interest is again stirred, and we are carried back to the days—

"... when Legions in their pride,
Defiling o'er the mountain side,
Marched up the Tweed's green wooded vale
With banners full spread to the gale."

BADDINSGILL.

The headwaters of the Lyne have now been gathered into a lake in the hollow of the hills, supplying Bathgate and district with water, and although such works always bear the impress of their origin, yet Nature has so exercised her beautifying influence in alliance with man's engineering skill that the simple grandeur of the Pentland landscape has been much enhanced by this wide stretch of gleaming waters and alluring bays. Subtle and magical, too, are the shadows and reflections of the peaks cast by sunshine and fleeting cloud when the waters are still.

After passing Cairnmuir, Baddinsgill (in 1376 spelt " Baudynisgill " and " Baldonisgill "—supposed to be a corruption of Baldwin's Gill), Wakefield, and Stony-path, Lyne flows through Linton Roderick, passes stately Spitalhaugh, for long the residence of Sir James R. Ferguson, surgeon to the Prince Consort, and on to Romanno, Newlands, and Drochil, a district rich in antiquarian and literary lore of the eighteenth century. Rich also with the memory of many a worthy of long ago, whose fame is enshrined in the poetical effusions of the local doctor, Dr. Pennecuik, a much-loved personality, who was born in 1652 and died in 1722.

The verse-inspiring powers of " Lady Effie's ale " is celebrated in the doctor's poetical correspondence with William Clerk, advocate. " Ale both stout and brown " is referred to in Allan Ramsay's *Gentle Shepherd* as being obtained at West Linton ; and if we accept the Pentland Hills as " Pictland " Hills, we may be sure that the Picts brewed there the famous " heather ale."

The weavers' cob and shuttle were heard in Linton from early times ; the village was also famous for its cobblers. A deep silence comes at nightfall when blinds are drawn and doors shut and the narrow streets deserted, and if you listen you will hear, in between the keen airs that come whispering down from the heights and the crooning lullaby of the Lyne, the tap, tap, tapping of the cobblers ; but it fades away, like the last of the cobbler fraternity, of whom tradition says that he simply disappeared, and from that moment all knowledge of him ceased.

Gipsies also abounded in great numbers in the middle of the seventeenth century. In 1677 two Gipsy clans —the Faws and Shaws—travelling from Haddington Fair, met and fought two other clans—the Baillies and Browns—at Romanno. Those who were not killed or wounded were arrested by the Laird of Romanno and lodged in Peebles Tolbooth, and reported to the Privy Council. Their arms, money, and gold rings were confiscated, and after trial old Robert Shaw and three of his sons were hanged in the Grassmarket, and their clothed bodies thrown into an open grave in Greyfriars Churchyard. The body of the youngest went amissing, and it remained a mystery as to whether it had been stolen for the surgeons, or whether life had revived in the boy again and he had made his escape. Six years later the doctor built a dovecot to commemorate the " Polymachy," with this inscription :

> " The field of Gipsy blood which here you see
> A shelter for the harmless dove shall be."

The church and manse of Newlands are situated on the banks of the Lyne. Laird Brown of Newhall, writing in the early nineteenth century, remarked that " the minister's abode was well calculated to divert his attention from terrestrial to celestial objects. Indeed, he is forced to direct it almost perpendicularly, for bare hills rise behind him, in front is a decayed timber bridge over the dull and weedy Lyne, and steep naked hills as high and close to him as those behind. When he turns for amusement to the right," continues the laird, " he finds the once joyous inn—Cant's Walls—now deserted. When he seeks for consolation on his left, the church-yard at his elbow, with its old ruinated church, crumbling tombstones, defaced epitaphs, sand-glasses, skulls, shank-bones, tears, and *memento moris*, admonish him to look up for comfort from above. Even when he shrinks into his manse with its little old-fashioned windows, the scene is equally dark, dank, and joyless!" The Laird of Newhall, like the doctor who became Laird of Romanno, was fond of his joke, but the poems of both pay tribute to the high esteem in which they held the minister of Newlands.

The noted Romanno Terraces, similar to those on the eastern slope of Dunsyre Hill, have been much discussed by geologists and antiquarians, and the latest account of their origin and purpose is the subject of a paper by Mr. W. W. T. Hannah, of The Whim, Lamancha, to the Antiquarian Society, Edinburgh, and his conclusion is that the Terraces were constructed in prehistoric times for the purpose of cultivation.

The green swelling hills of Tweeddale never fail to thrill us with their story ; and the traveller may be pardoned if, when he comes upon the dark ruin of Drochil Castle on Lyne, he imagines that here is a relic of an ancient Border story. But away back in 1564 the once great and powerful Earl of Morton planned to have a palace here, where, far from the scheming and intrigue of Court, he might at last find rest amidst the peaceful quietude of the hills. Alas, it was not to be, for he fell from his high estate, first, as Lord High Chancellor of Scotland, being implicated in Rizzio's murder, and then, as Regent to the young king, falling under the queen's displeasure. He was found guilty of being privy to the conspiracy against Darnley, and of being " art and part " in the murder. It is a tradition that the Maiden, or French guillotine, by which he died in 1581, was a model made by himself, a copy of one first seen by him at Halifax.

There was probably a tower at Drochil before there was a castle, as two years before the castle building was begun a lease of lands at Nether Drochil in 1562, in favour of one John Bold, describes the tenant as " indweller in the Towyr." In 1584–85 the then Earl of Morton was one of the rebel lords of James VI., and was ordered to deliver up " Drochellis " to the king's officers ; and in 1600 certain lords and lairds were ordered to reside in their houses near the Borders for the repression and pursuit of Border thieves, and among others William, Earl of Morton, his son and baillies, were appointed to reside in the " Castle of Drochellis."

The ruin is worth visiting as a specimen of sixteenth-century building and arrangement, and the initials " J. D." (James Douglas) with a fetterlock as Warden of the Borders, are carved over the south entrance, while " J. E. O. M." (James, Earl of Morton) may be seen built into the gable-end of one of the farm buildings. The present farmhouse was built about 1824. The last time I visited the ruin the spacious entrance hall was being used as a sheep pen.

In 1755 the principal occupation of the inhabitants of the village of Lyne was the shoeing of horses, the

WHERE LYNE JOINS TWEED.

sharpening of farm implements, and the making of nails.
As early as 1208 there is mention of a grain mill at Lyne,
which probably stood in the Haugh beside Hallyne,
where in 1550 the Baron's Court was held.   The millers
of Lyne were famous for centuries all over the countryside, and a certain miller, who was also a millwright
there late in the eighteenth century, was described " as
keeping in repair the greater part of the machinery in
Tweeddale."   The lint mill near Lyne Toll Bridge
ceased when lint was no longed used as thatch.

The kirk and the mill were the two principal places
in every old Scots village.   So it was in Lyne.   The
date of the first kirk or chapel goes back to the days
of antiquity.   The present small building that stands
upon an eminence, and is prominent in the landscape,
is modern, but the pulpit, which was brought from
Holland, was presented by Lady Yester in 1644.   It
is recorded that when winter storms visited the valley
few members of the congregation could gather together
for public worship, and the minister would frequently
hold the service in his kitchen, which was the largest
and most comfortable room in the manse, " where a
convenient pause in the service was sometimes usefully
prolonged to give his servant an opportunity to stir the
fire and the pot."

Prior to 1804, when Megget had neither church nor
school, the minister and schoolmaster of Lyne parish,
which was united with Megget, visited the farm folks
from time to time preaching and teaching, and it was
not uncommon for the minister to start from Lyne on
a Sunday morning at six o'clock, and return the same
evening after having walked or ridden to Megget and
back—some twenty-six miles.   A story is told of Mr.

Johnston, the bachelor minister of Lyne and Megget
for sixty years from 1728, regarding the form of marriage
service used by him.   It was not exactly of an encourag-
ing nature to those who had decided to make the great
adventure, for it began, " My freends, marriage is a
curse to many, a blessing to a few, a lottery to all.
Wull ye ventur' ? "

Within sight of Lyne Kirk lies Sheriffmuir, bounded
by Tweed's white pebbly shore, which was used as an
exercise ground for the Tweeddale militia prior to the
Union.   It was the place appointed by the sheriff, hence
its name, but the chief place of meeting was the King's
Muir at Peebles, where the great " Wapon-shawing "
took place in 1627, when 294 horsemen and 10 footmen
were present.

As we climb the hills behind the kirk to view the
Roman Camp, we pause to catch a view of Tweed's
clear rippling stream sweeping steadily and grandly
down the wide valley, flanked on each side with lofty
hills of green pastures that climb to the sky.   Planta-
tions, enclosures, and farm steadings dot the fair landscape, where Newposso (Wester Dawick), Stobo, and
Barns, and many another home of Border story, lie
beaking in the sun.   Here indeed is a land of real
romance.

The whole of this hilly pastoral countryside through
which flows Lyne Water is rich in scenic, historic, and
antiquarian lore, with many a fascinating viewpoint for
those who love the high hills, where the wayfarer, be he
artist in literature or in colours, or just a rambler in
search of impressions, will find many a beautiful and
inspiring scene in each revolving season.

Chapter V

A NIGHT ON THE HILLS

THE elderly booking-office clerk at the quiet suburban station was too much astonished to say anything—he just murmured ; he could not remember ever having been asked for so many tickets at such an hour, even on a Saturday night : but as each of us made our request he began to understand—thirty tickets to a small one-sided station in a sylvan glade near the Pentland Hills. He was perhaps a little annoyed at having to take down his shutters after having put them up. " There's no sayin' what these young fellows are up to nowadays ; times are changed, times are changed," and he was glad when he handed out the last ticket and the train steamed into the station ; business for the week was ended so far as he was concerned.

We were a happy, smiling crowd, full of the enthusiasm and boisterous gaiety of youth, bound for the open spaces of freedom, off to spend a night on the Pentland hilltops, and to see the sunrise ! Oh ! the joy of it. No wonder we thrilled at the thought, shook the hand of our nearest companion, and gave expression to our merriment in song. The train journey passed unheeded. We could see the hills through the darkening shadows, and our thoughts settled upon the rim of outstanding peaks.

Filing out of the station, the leader gave directions as

to the route to be followed, and soon we were stepping out briskly with the energy of youth, eager for the upward climb. Firstly, there was the hard road, then the path across the fields and through the woods, and lastly, and all through the night, the pastures green and the heather, good to walk over, soft to lie down upon.

Before beginning the climb to the head of the glen we paused to view the illuminated city that lay behind us. Rows of lighted streets stretched out to suburban places; in the centre of the city brilliant lights clustered here and there, and much merriment ensued as we endeavoured to locate the various landmarks. Here in the glen we were sheltered from the westerly gale that raged above us, and as the path wound gradually upwards we welcomed every breeze that found its way down through this corridor in the hills. The exercise was exhilarating, the wind was fresh and cool upon the cheeks, and already we were beginning to feel the tonic effects of the Pentland air.

" Good-morning, everybody," exclaimed the humorist, who had been carrying his watch in his hand for the last five minutes. " Think of all the thousands down below asleep in their warm beds," said another. " Lucky beggars," ejaculated Tired Tim. " They won't see the sunrise," cried Eager Will. " Nor shall we," sobbed Doleful Doughty, and the rest was lost in a gust of wind.

Half an hour's climb brought us to the head of the Drovers' Glen, where the view of the peaks is unsurpassed ; and under the bield of a dry-stane dyke we made our first camp. " Supper or breakfast, which ? " inquired our wit. " It must be both in one," he answered, " because I've got some of each between these two chunks of bread." We fared sumptuously—

we had been duly forewarned as to the necessity of bringing food with us—and we were happy. Then we had a chorus, the chief conducting vigorously to keep himself warm.

What was to be done between now and sunrise ? We had sufficient energy to take us to the Cairn Hills and back again before 4.30. Unfortunately the leader's " surprise item " proved to be a delusion. He had counted upon a still, warm summer night, and had hoped to entertain us with conundrums as to the varied sounds of birds and beasts among the hills at night time, but he had not reckoned upon so tempestuous a night, and the only sounds that could be heard were the varying tones of the winds roving among the hills and valleys, and whistling through the grassy bents and heather.

" What about a scamper over the top of the Law above the old castle ? " " Right," chorused a score of voices, " and we'll leave our packs behind us," for youth is eager for any fresh adventure, and discards everything that is superfluous. It was just what we required, for the stiff climb to the summit helped to quieten our boisterous spirits and prepare us for the feast upon the hilltop.

But again we reckoned without the gale. It was with difficulty we could stand erect, and we sought the shelter of the cairn. Here we rested for a little, and with the mind's eye we pictured to ourselves the King's Hill upon which the Bruce had stood to view the chase of the white faunch deer, and granted to the victor—Sir William St. Clair—a charter of " all our land in the Moor of Pentlande with pertinents." We saw the monks from Mount Lothian wending their way to the chapel of Saint Katherine, before the days of the Bruce ; we heard the song of the Covenanters rising upon the clear, frosty air, then the clatter of hoofs and the clash of arms upon the slopes of Turnhouse ; we dreamed of the life of the ancient Britons in the forts on the hillsides beneath us in the valley, whose story will never be told.

Yet the weird grandeur of that view from the hilltop we shall not forget, for the gorge at the head of the Logan valley was as the crater of a volcano, belching forth a continuous stream of smoke clouds, dark as Erebus, which shot out across the hills with hurricane fury. Suddenly, for a moment, the clouds parted above us, all the woods and valleys and waters were lit by a shining light, and we hailed the moon with a burst of song, whose refrain floated away into space, " Moon, moon, moon ! "

As we crossed the valley between the peaks, in which in olden times there was a farm called "The Leeps," known to Renwick, the Covenanter, we were forced to find shelter from a squall of wind and rain behind a dry-stane dyke, and, closely packed together, we found it warm and comfortable. Youth loves variety, and there was abundance of it to please us all in the rough, stormy weather of this midsummer night. Later we had another spell of climbing, and found shelter on a height, from which we obtained an uninterrupted view of the city. That there should be so many street lamps burning in Auld Reekie at 3 a.m. on a Sabbath morn in midsummer seemed strange, but we did not cavil. We enjoyed the illuminations, the moving lights of belated motor-cars upon the Biggar road, the strong beams from the mariners' warning light on Inchkeith, and the twinkling lights across the Forth.

Then suddenly every light disappeared as enveloping

banks of mist spread over the hills. Some of the party
thought this must be the end of all things, and, com-
fortably wedging themselves in among their fellows,
feigned that they were asleep, oblivious of everything.
But others were quietly watching the pageant of the
clouds across the sky—the fleets of Heaven that know
no haven—and the mist did not long survive in the
windy gale. We were all very quiet now, the force of
the elements, terrible at times in their sublimity, the
wonder of the scurrying clouds, the weird vision of the
hilltops among the flying mists, the inky blackness of
the valleys, the intermittent " soughin' " of the wintry
wind—all brought another spirit upon us, and we found
other songs that were good to sing, and attuned our
spirits to the spirit of the elements. The strange, sweet
harmony of a hymn by Cowper, the poet of men made
calm and serene as they walked in darkness, guided by
a light, rose around us ; and as we watched, the heavens
eastwards were becoming lighter, though the wind
ceased not its fury. Once, during a lull in the storm,
we heard a lark singing, but it was as a voice in the
wilderness, for none of the other birds was heard, and
not even chanticleer proclaiming the dawn made his
voice heard in the storm.

Was our " sunrise " then to be a disappointment—
had we witnessed all that was to be seen of the wonder of the breaking of the day—only a few fissures in
the darkened clouds, lit with a cold blue whiteness,
and a pink glow athwart the heavens ? Disappointed,
we turned to go. The mist blew up again, bringing with
it a stinging rain ; then it cleared once more, and we
found ourselves about to descend.

When about a hundred yards from the top wonderful

things began to happen. Brilliant lights and gorgeous colours flamed in the sky, and sixty eyes looked upwards, while every voice was stilled.

Here we were sheltered from the gale, and in quietness we could marvel at the scene before us. The colours glowed and spread, winged clouds in fantastic shapes passed in quick succession, the rim of the giant ball appeared and grew in stately grace till the whole circumference came into view, a faint curtain of haze passed across it, and brighter colours appeared upon the edges of the upper strata of dark cloud, then the light burst in fullest radiance to shine but for a brief space. The battle of the elements was unequal, the light grew dim again, burst forth afresh, then faded away.

The chief addressed us, and thanked the leader, and the leader said something in reply about " experiences that we never forget, that become part of our being, that direct us to a truer worship of Him who is the author of it all." Grouped upon the steep hillside we stood, with heads erect and faces towards the sunrising, a company of strong, manly fellows, who had seen a vision that touched the heart. Then very quietly some one called—a verse of Stracathro—and the hillside resounded with the swelling sound of the old Psalm tune —of words that spoke of consciousness of the Highest, in whose house would be our dwelling for evermore. . . . His house in the hills . . . where clean hands and a pure heart are the passport. . . .

It was a long line of silent, stalwart lads that marched in Indian file down the winding hill road and through the field paths homewards in the glowing light of an early Sabbath morn. We had seen the sunrise. We had spent a night on the hills.

ROMANNO TERRACES.

Chapter VI

HARLAW MOOR

THE moorland of Harlaw and Auchencorth, cradled in the bosom of green rolling hills, lies between Penicuik and Linton Roderick, bounded on the west by the Edinburgh–Biggar road and the higher reaches of the North Esk River, and on the east by the Leadburn–Romanno highway.

It is a wide and spacious tract, about six miles in length, and the farther we travel along the " Moor Road " from Penicuik the more wonderful becomes the panorama in front of us, unfolding to our view the green sweeping hills of Pentland and the Meldons, the Broughton Heights and the Pyket Stane, Broadlaw, Coulter Fell and Tinto Tap.

At the southern end of the moor lie the lands of Whitfield, which at one time belonged to the son of Drummond of Hawthornden, while the adjoining village of Linton was connected with the Comyns prior to the days of Bruce. Of this family was " The Red Comyn," who claimed the crown of Scotland, but later supported Baliol. It was his son—The Red Comyn number two —who was killed by Bruce in Dumfries. Early in the fourteenth century the Morton branch of the Douglas family acquired lands in Linton, and gradually came to own nearly the whole parish. The " Knight of Liddes-

dale " was, of course, a Douglas, and also owned lands
in and around Linton, while the Pentland Hills were
frequently his headquarters, from which he sallied forth
upon his daring exploits.

Brunstane Castle, on the western edge of the moor,
is a traditional hiding-place of George Wishart, the
martyr, and Penicuik House has pleasant memories of
Sir Walter, for he was a frequent visitor to " that fair
dome where suit is paid by blast of bugle free," and the
" White Rose of Scotland " was none other than Lady
Mary Clerk.

The moor to-day is but a grazing ground for sheep
and a home for wild game, but in other days coal, iron,
limestone, and blue clay marl were worked. Stone was
quarried at Deepsykehead and Marfield, and farmers
from as far away as Annandale came to the moor for
the white sandstone used in sharpening scythes. Peat is
still worked. The Marfield mineral spring flows into the
Esk; and there was a day when Marfield Loch had
" life and spirit " derived from a West Indian pirate
yawl picked up in the Gulf of Mexico by a Clyde-bound
vessel, and presented to Robert D. C. Brown, the Laird of
Newhall, as a curiosity, who kept it in the loch. There
was also a day when the Harbour Craig was a refuge
and a meeting-place of Covenanters, and while Habbie's
Howe has associations in the minds of poets and singers
with fairies, Carlops with witches, Newhall gardens with
ancient tragedy, and Newlands with Gipsies, the moor
itself has many stories and traditions associated with
it. Few of those who engaged in the illicit distilling
on the moor were ever found out. So tradition tells.
When the search became too active, the apparatus disappeared.

Interesting as are the old legends of the moor, and the historical antiquities of castles and old country houses, it is the æsthetic and romantic call of the open moorland and towering hills that thrills us. At no time does the moor invite to sweet reflection more than in the twilight hour of a summer evening, when amidst the silence we listen to the voices of the wild—the cry of the green-crested lapwing, the cooing of doves, the bleating of sheep, the lowing of cattle. The surrounding moorland seems spirit-haunted ; it is the hour of dusk before the curtain of night falls ; between the gloamin' and the mirk—when enchantment lies around us like a spell.

It is from the moor that we view the most attractive outline of the Pentlands, and in the summer twilight they radiate ethereal beauty. Up the slopes of Turnhouse and Carnethy creep the blue shadows, and above the Spital Hills and the Kips pass the ever-changing trailing clouds, while the weather-gleam shining above the Black Hill and Scald Law makes them more mysterious, till at last they melt into indistinctness and fade away. But by the time the voyaging clouds have polished the sky, the azure ·vault is lit by the crescent moon and by the stars that sing all through the summer night.

Intimacy with the hills is gained by frequent communing in walking and wandering over the heights and valleys, and among the nooks and crannies, yet there is a certain subtle joy in beholding the hills and their homely features from the old Moor Road, and perhaps it is just this and the refreshing and exhilarating hill air that bring Walkers as well as motorists to the Old Road. And in their season the larks are always singing above the moor, so high as to be almost out of sight, and seeing they sing for the joy of living they needs must know the secret of life, for deep down at the root of all things is joy, and from the highest heavens the larks send forth the praise of it, soaring to bring down love with a song from Heaven to the mate on the nest beneath.

There is another artist at work. The sky pictures on such a wide canvas play an important part in our enjoyment of the moor. The aspects of the hills change continually as the light plays over the pyramidical groups and searches the hollows of every depression, for it is a landscape that is pastoral and pleasant, where smooth rounded hills in velvet verdure, with flowing outlines, overlap and melt into each other.

If we would know the moor intimately we must visit her in all her varied moods, and experience not only the joys of summer days, but also the wonder and the awesomeness of the place in the blackness of a winter night, with the wind soughing through the remnants of the pine forest and over the waving bents. Tradition has it that the witches between Forth and Tweed claimed the moor as their very own, and here held such revelry and played such pranks as far surpassed all that Tam o' Shanter ever saw in the Land o' Burns.

" All seasons shall be sweet to thee," sings the poet, and there is joy to be found in the moor in the frosty nights of winter when the landscape lies white under a deep blue sky, and moon and stars make night visible. There is then a stillness in the moor that holds us with a strange fascination, for at such times there seems nought between earth and heaven ; space is annihilated, the sounds of earth are still, and the shining of the stars above the snow-white peaks infuses strange new life into

THE HILLS FROM HARLAW MOOR.

the imagination. The starry sky is linked with silver chains to the midnight silence of the hills, and spirits converse on every hill, in every vale. A new meaning comes to us in Wordsworth's lines :

> " The silence that is in the starry sky,
> The sleep that is among the lonely hills."

The moor has many secrets. But it is when we visit the moorland in the dawn of a summer morning that she reveals herself in her most intimate mood—when the song birds with full abandon hail the rising sun ; when the wild things leave the heather and gambol on the smooth white road ; when the grey dawn skies are soft as the eyes of the gazelle, and pearly clouds like angels' wings float in the azure sky. It is then that Harlaw Moor becomes a fairyland, and, with Peter Pan, we fain would stroke the conies as they gambol at their play.

Chapter VII

LOVERS OF THE OPEN AIR

" When they saw the men of Rome walking for the pleasure of Walking they thought they must be mad."

STRABO.

How often we are thrilled with the beauty of the world and of Nature's surpassing loveliness in her alternate pause and change; and yet, while all this feast of Nature's bounty has been there from the beginning of time, it is little more than two centuries since man began to write about these things. In recent years there has been a revival of such writings, together with the re-discovery of the joys to be found in walking over hill path and country road and the unknown, unfrequented places of our Island. This department of Nature writing and topography has opened up a wide field ; wise discrimination is necessary.

In Scotland, Allan Ramsay, whose pastoral comedy, *The Gentle Shepherd*, was first published in 1725 ; James Thomson (1700–48), whose poem of *The Seasons* marked a new era in English literature so far as the description of Nature in poetry was concerned ; and in France, Rousseau (1712–78) may be said to represent the pioneers in their respective countries. One does not forget, of course, that there were poetical descriptions of Nature in the ancient world and in the

Middle Ages, or that in the days following upon the writings of the pioneers mentioned, the circle became greatly widened by the writings of Cowper, Coleridge, Wordsworth, Keats, and Shelley, and all true poets since their day, in whom the feeling for Nature may now be said to be a common possession. In literature dealing with appreciation of scenery in its grander and awe-inspiring form—the scenery of mountains—Wordsworth and Sir Walter Scott were the founders of a school that has never ceased to grow, one which numbers among its members not only poets and Nature lovers, but also novelists and even men of science, for Sir Archibald Geikie's *Landscape in History* is a noteworthy contribution, in which the essays " Landscape and Imagination " and " Landscape and Literature " are specially interesting to hill lovers.

It is good and profitable at times to go back to the works of Sir Walter Scott, whose descriptive and critical powers are still unrivalled ; of James Hogg, " the Ettrick Shepherd " ; of Professor John Wilson, " Christopher North," and of Principal John Campbell Shairp, to name but a few, that we may better appreciate the writings of the present day.

How close to the heart the Ettrick Shepherd comes in his intimate description of Nature ! Familiarity with the hills never made them commonplace or lose their power of stimulating his imagination. Eight hours out of every twenty-four " i' the open air, wi' heaven's wind and rain or hail and sleet—blessed be the Hand that sends them—blashing against me on the hill."

The mysterious sights and sounds among the hills in the varied seasons, for which the Hill-walker is ever on the alert, were dear to him—the trailing mists among

the tops, the glories of the dawn, the pearly grey of the
weather-gleam along the outline of his Border hills and
the soul-subduing peace of the gloaming brought to
him the wonder and the might of the Unseen, and in his
writings there is the power to thrill and subdue us into
the realm in which he, at his best, was so much at home.
With him we would sing :

" Be mine to sing of visions that have been,
    And cherish hope of visions yet to be,
Of mountains clothed in everlasting green,
    Of silver torrent and of shadowy tree.
Be mine the faith that spurns the bourn of time ;
    The soul whose eye can future glories see ;
The converse here with things of purer clime,
And hope above the stars that soars on wings sublime."

" Christopher North," happy in his constraining love
of Nature, would walk through the hills all night till
the dawn flushed over the top, and find in the experience
the very elixir of life.

" Go up among the mountains when the storm
    Of midnight howls, but go in that wild mood,
    When the soul loves tumultuous solitude.

.   .   .   .   .   .

Oh ! worship thou the visions then made known,
    While sable glooms round Nature's temple roll,
    And her dread anthem peals into thy soul."

The fresh smell of the grass and the heather after rain,
and the atmosphere and tang of the moorland hills come
as a tonic from some of his little-read poetry.

Scott, Hogg, and Wilson knew the Pentlands well,
and frequently met together as members of the Six Foot
Club, whose outings into the country usually included

supper at the inn of Hunters' Tryst. Scott's residence at Lasswade, and Wilson's at Roslin, made it easy for them to reach the hills, and they had a common friend in the Laird of Woodhouselee. The story is told that one day as " North " strode along a hillside he was overheard by some farm workers in a field near by singing at the pitch of his voice, and one of the " knowing ones " remarked to his companion, " Eh, man, man, but the hill hunger's bad on him the day."

In Principal Shairp we have one who was loved wherever he went, never more happy than when wandering among the hills and spending a night with a shepherd in his "but-an'-ben " ; and if the daylight were not sufficient to satisfy his great heart yearnings for the solitudes of the glens and the high places, there was starlight and the shining of the moon in which to walk ; and so there came these writings of his which every hillman and Nature lover treasures, especially those of the older generation—*Glen Dessary and other Poems, The Poetic Interpretation of Nature, Aspects of Poetry,* etc., proclaiming an intense love of Nature, and the deep feeling for the complement which outward Nature affords to the mind of man. To what far spaces does the mind travel in reading the following verse, and what joy and refreshing it brings to the heart :

> " Thanks to that Glen ; its scenery blends
>   With childhood's most ideal hour,
>   When Highland hills I made my friends,
>   First owned their beauty, felt their power."

Byron's love of the mountains was born at Ballater when he was eight years of age, and the older he grew the stronger became his attachment to wild and stern

aspects of Nature. The thrilling power, strength, and everlastingness of the high hills found a response in his heart and became part of himself, and with the true Walker he proclaims there is no such thing as solitude :

" To climb the trackless mountain all unseen,
   With the wild flock that never needs a fold ;
Alone o'er steeps, and foaming falls to lean,
   This is not solitude, 'tis but to hold
Converse with Nature's charm and view her stores
   unrolled."

The " power of the hills " could not be said to inspire or influence Shakespeare, to whom the forest was a favourite. " Mountain raptures," Principal Shairp points out, " had to be dumb for two centuries before it found utterance in English song." Neither did Burns come under its spell. The mountains and high hills with their grandeur and glory and the voices of the vasty solitudes did not inspire the muse of " Scotia's Bard." But of his love of the pastoral scenes in the glens and haughs, and along the valleys and streams of his native Ayrshire, and of the Nith, and the sea coast, we have ample evidence. Yet we have expressions of the mind of Burns showing his susceptibility to the wild moods of Nature also, in which he found a certain comfort and solace. This is referred to in his letters and in his dirge, *Winter*. Writing to Robert Riddell, he says :

" I take peculiar pleasure in the season of winter more than the rest of the year. This, I believe, may be partly owing to my misfortunes giving my mind a melancholy cast, but there is something even in the

' Mighty tempest and the hoary waste,
   Abrupt and deep, stretched o'er the buried earth,'

which raises the mind to a serious sublimity favourable
to everything great and noble. There is scarcely any
earthly object gives me more—I don't know if I should
call it pleasure, but something which exalts me, something which enraptures me—than to walk in the sheltered
side of a wood or high plantation, in a cloudy winter
day, and hear a stormy wind howling among the trees,
and raving o'er the plain. It is my best season for
devotion; my mind is rapt up in a kind of enthusiasm
to Him who, in the pompous language of Scripture,
' walks on the wings of the wind.' "

It is not alone to the mind beset with melancholy that
this feeling of exaltation comes. Winter is the ideal
time for walking, and to the youthful heart rejoicing in
its exuberant vigour and care-free abandon there is
great attraction in the stormy elements—within reason
—among the hills in winter. We become one with the
spirit of the wind as it whistles and shouts from hill to
hill, buffeting us with rollicking glee and titanic laughter,
and we join willingly in its jovial play. There is real
philosophy in the Highlander's remark, " A fine day,
but coorse."

The old Scots idea of the wind and the storm being
evil and sinister is gone. Burns listens to it on the
lee side of a wood, and speaks of it " howling " and
" raving " ; to Stevenson it is " hell " ; but to modern
hill walkers and mountain climbers there is an intimacy
in the wind and storm which sings, however exultingly
and boisterously, among the trees, laughs in the valleys
like a giant, and whistles and screeches along the rocky
hillsides—expressions of its liberty and sublime power
reminding us of the poetical description in Scripture of
the mountains and hills as breaking forth into singing

and all the trees of the field clapping their hands, a mood equally applicable to devotion and exaltation.

The works of Rousseau are not so well known. This philosophic writer of the eighteenth century is interesting to present-day lovers of the open air and the open road in that he had an intense feeling for Nature, and was a Walker. That amiable French critic, Sainte-Beuve, writes in one of his *Causeries du Lundi* (1850) that Rousseau was the first to write of Nature in France —" from him dates with us the feeling for Nature." Like Chateaubriand, Rousseau could turn from the extremes of gaiety and noise to silence and melancholy, could sit aloof and contemplate the fleeting clouds, or listen to the rain falling on the foliage, and then, dropping into reverie, soliloquize that there was nothing more poetical in the freshness of its passions than a heart of sixteen ; the morning of life is like the morning of the day, full of purity, images, and harmonies. Sainte-Beuve emphasizes the freshness and the new life that Rousseau infused into the literature of France. It was said he was the first to put " green " into French literature. " It was the first time that I had green before my windows," he writes in recollection of the place where he was boarded out in his childhood. He was affected by the song of birds, the beauty of the day, the softness of the landscape. All this ecstasy which contemplation had brought to him he introduced into French literature, which until then (1731) had been dissolute and materialistic. Nothing like this, for instance, had before been described. Writing of a certain excursion, he says, " Everything seemed to contribute to the happiness of the day. It had rained shortly before ; no dust, and the rivulets very full ; a little fresh breeze was stirring the leaves, the air was pure, the horizon was cloudless, serenity reigned in the sky as in our hearts. We had our dinner at a peasant's, sharing it with the family, who blessed us heartily. These poor Savoyards are such good people."

It was quite a new departure in literature in those days to write of walking—" travelling on foot." Rousseau in his *Confessions* writes, " Never have I thought so much, existed so much, lived so much, in fact been so much myself, if I may say so, as in those journeys which I have made alone, and on foot." Again he tells us that it was only when travelling on foot in fine weather, in a beautiful country, without being hurried, that thoughts and inspirations came which would not come when seated in his study. " Ideas," he said, " come when *they* please, not when *I* please."

Of walking he says, " There is something in walking that stirs and quickens my ideas. I can hardly think when I remain in one place ; my body must be on the move to set my mind going. The sight of the country, the succession of agreeable views, the open air, the big appetite, the good health I win by walking, the freedom of the inn, the absence of everything that reminds me of my situation, all this loosens my soul, and gives me a greater audacity to think."

Again, take this extract from his description of the night he spent at the sign of the " Beautiful Star," near Lyons, as revealing the natural Rousseau : " I lay down voluptuously on the ledge of a sort of recess or false door let into the wall of a terrace, the tester of my bed was formed by the tree tops ; a nightingale was just overhead, and I went to sleep to its song ; my slumbers were sweet, my awakening was still more so. It was broad daylight; my eyes on opening saw the water, the verdure, a wonderful landscape. I got up and shook myself; I felt hungry; I wended my way gaily to the town resolved to spend two pieces of six blanks that I still had left in a good breakfast."

This is not unlike Hazlitt: " Give me the clear blue sky over my head and the green turf beneath my feet, a winding road before me and a three hours' march to dinner, and then to thinking." Every one will not agree, of course, that the aim of the Walker is to induce thinking. On the contrary, to enjoy country or hill walking one must surrender oneself wholly to the influences and impulses of Nature around one, and while enjoying the new life that comes with exercise, allow the finer feelings to be influenced by that gentle spirit that lives in every breeze. It is interesting to note that Hazlitt frequently quotes Rousseau, and always with admiration. He commends the *Confessions* as the most valuable of all his writings. It was Rousseau's *Nouvelle Héloïse* that he tells us he enjoyed at the inn at Llangollen over a bottle of sherry and a cold chicken, after a day in the open.

Our own R. L. S. had many experiences like this in the Cevennes, along with Modestine, and it is refreshing to re-read in this book his philosophy of travel, of friendship, of nights under the stars " at God's green Caravanserai," of his solemn glee as he watches the day break over the mountains of Vivarais: "I heard the runnel with delight; I looked around for something beautiful and unexpected, but the still black pines, the hollow glade and munching ass remained unchanged in figure. Nothing had altered but the light, and that indeed shed over all a spirit of life and breathing peace, and moved me to a strange exhilaration." Then, his importunate fancy, that somehow he felt in some one's debt for this night's lodging in God's open house, and it pleased him in a half-laughing way to leave pieces of money on the turf as he went along, hoping that it would fall into hands that merited it. R. L. S. wrote his book a hundred years after Rousseau died.

Walkers may compare their fancies with moderns such as Leslie Stephen, G. M. Trevelyan, Stephen Graham, or Grayson, and find joy in reflection upon the Nature writings of Eden Phillpotts with his charming pictures of moorland and cloudland, sunset and dawn, and one does not require to be a mountaineer to appreciate the heights to which communion with Nature may attain in Geoffrey Winthrop Young's great book, *On High Hills*, or feel the grip of truth in his poetry that speaks to all lovers of the hills:

> " Take them, O heart,
> The joy of comrades and the thrill of strife,
>   Who has the hills for friend
>   Has a good-speed to end
>   His path of lonely life
> And wings of golden memory to depart;
>   Take them for love, true heart."

Chapter VIII

PENTLAND POETS

IT is when the refreshing winds of spring are blowing and chasing cloud shadows across sunlit hillsides and glens that we long to stand upon the tops of the high hills. There the true perspective of life returns, we find our soul, we are whole again, all the world is fresh and fair, and " on the brow is the calm of wide spaces reflected, in the eye the light of long distance un-broken."

So it seems to-day as we stand upon the hill-tops look-ing across to the Kips and Scald Law. It is a view of the Highlands in miniature, and the bracing air fills us with a vigour and a joy that make us glad—a gladness reflected in the health of the countenance. The hills reveal us to ourselves, and interpret the meaning of life. In such circumstances distance travelled does not count ; it is interest in life that counts. And the hills help us to a true assessment of values. Our love of life, and life of love, are interpreted afresh in the joyous call of the hills. So have the hills begotten a literary spirit that has seldom been without a voice.

Always the hills become identified with the life and thought of those who dwell among them. To Baron Sir John Clerk of Penicuik in the early eighteenth century the environs of the Esk were the Tempe of Scotland, where her poets were inspired and gained immortality. To Robert D. C. Brown, the lawyer laird of Newhall, Carlops, Scald Law resembled Parnassus— it was the Scalds' or Poets' Hill, with a fountain at its base, a Heliconian spring, a rivulet paying tribute to the North Esk for its poets and poetic scenery. Near by were the Cairn Hill and Druids' Hill, and the Harpers' Hill, the hill of the Scalds in their character as musicians, while the two Kips were Helicon and Cithæron. Classical learning and literary aspiration went together. Did the laird desire to write of Mary, Scotland's queen, as in *Henry, Lord Darnley, King of Scots, an Historical Tragedy*, published in 1829, then the queen must have a Pentland association, so in the quiet evening, as she travels by the Pentland Hills, she hears " the warblings soft and shrill of shepherd's pipe." On she rides to Carlops to visit the Carline by the Rocks—there to learn in detail her tragic destiny ; and who more fit than the Carlops Witch to spin the tale ?

To him the district was the Arcadia of Scotland, not only because of the smoothness and verdure of the spacious hills and the pastoral character of the inhabitants and scenery, but also for the poetic inspiration that seemed to abound amidst these surroundings.

Dr. Pennecuik, the Linton doctor, fell under the spell, and wrote his humorous poems of early eighteenth-century life and manners in the intervals between attending patients and botanizing, and he is believed to have supplied Allan Ramsay with the plot of *The Gentle Shepherd*. He also required scope for his jocular raillery, and so to delight his friends he draws a picture of them all, gathering at Linton, well horsed and jacked ready for the fray, and so indites a " Panegyrick " upon the Royal Army in Scotland, and particularly upon the Troops of Tweeddale and Forest, gentlemen convened by Royal Authority in May 1685 under command of the Laird of Drummelzier, to suppress what was called Argyle's Rebellion.

Or is it a simple vignette of a rural scene among the hills that the last of the old, cultured lairds, Dr. Horatio R. F. Brown, would give us ?—for Dr. Horatio, the friend of Symonds and R. L. S., loved the old domain with all his heart, although he lived much in Venice, where he died in 1926. Then it is a picture such as Jacques himself would have loved to paint. Up the ravine above Carlops Brig and the Old Mill, just below Fairliehope, the folds of the hills sloping rapidly down to the burn are filled with a gentle grey mist ; it is the time of sheep-dipping ; the bleating of the animals penned at the end of the dipper fills the glen with their long lament. Through the haze loom the figures of the shepherds, their mauve-coloured flannel shirts in perfect harmony with the whitey-yellow of the fleeces and the faint straw-yellow of the grassy hillsides. Not a word from the workers, but the sheep are seized by neck and rump, and held down in the dipping-trough, then a wild scramble with their forefeet on the slippery boards, and they rush into the upper pen, their warm bodies sending off vapour that blends and mingles with the natural mists of the glen. It is a sheep-dipping Pastoral of the Pentlands.

All that those writers sought to portray must centre round the hills that were their spacious home, green rounded hills that flowed into each other, where line and colour gave such dignity and beauty as made them a continual source of inspiration and delight, not only to the lairds, the doctors, and the literary men, but also to the shepherds, keepers, mole-catchers, weavers, and joiners. No one escaped the literary spirit of the countryside.

On several occasions Dr. Brown stayed at the Allan Ramsay Hotel in Carlops, where he loved to renew acquaintance with the older tenants on the estate, many of whom were greatly concerned to account for his long absences abroad. They knew that he was a man deeply learned in classical lore, and assumed that these studies were the reason for his residence in Italy, but he was somewhat amused one day to be greeted with the remark, " Weel, Mr. Broon, will ye be near finished with yer schoolin' yet ? " Another tenant, who dreamed dreams and saw visions in his " lanely bield " in the glen behind Newhall, and like his laird compiled verses and had them printed too, in the course of conversation remarked, " You know, Mr. Broon, I've never had a sicht o' ony o' yer books ! "

" I'll send you one, Andra," replied the laird.

" It'll no be written in Italian, will it ? "

" No, no."

" Then ye can send it to me, for I can read the warst English."

The laird never knew the old man's thoughts about the book, and he was satisfied to let the matter rest, because he had it in remembrance that when the old man's father was asked by the laird's father for a candid opinion of the verse of his grandfather, he got for answer, " Weel, Mr. Broon, I'm truly sorry to be compelled to state that the maist I can say o' them is that they're perfect trash ! "

Dr. Brown enjoyed the humours of the countryside ; he understood the Carlops folks and their ways, and was always ready for what he termed " the privy nip," which he described as " never long absent from the conversation of the shrewd dwellers in this upland unfrequented region," administered, as he believed, " in all affection and just to see what you are made of." Their curiosity about the laird's affairs took strange forms. " Would he be turned a Roman Catholic, do you think, seeing he's been living so long in Italy ? "—" Ask him, Tammas " ; and one day he was asked, but not directly— no, that would never do—and so, leading up to the subject, the appointed delegate made the apparently casual remark, " Weel, Mr. Broon, I canna abide the Virgin Mary," and then followed such a tense inspection of the laird's face that he almost felt the force of it as if it had been a blow. I fancy the laird would just smile. Like all scholars he was a quiet man, and practised the virtue of the golden rule about speech being silvern.

His insight into the lives and affections of the hill folk was powerful and sincere. " This upland country, high and bleak, barren almost in some places, takes a deep hold on the affections of its scanty population," he wrote, " its charm all the more potent for not being obvious. Talking with them, some chance expression will suddenly let you into their inner love ; you know that the space and dignity and distinction of their home have not passed before their eyes in vain ; a turn of phrase and you guess their passion for a June morning dewy in the glen or on the hill, for an autumn sunset flaming behind the western crests, and down the distant vale of Tweed."

NEWHALL, CARLOPS.

WANTON WA'S, CARLOPS.

Even in death they will not be divided from their
uplands. Dr. Brown has told the story of a cottar, old
and poor, whose homestead lay tucked away in one of
the unapproachable glens, and who fell ill and was taken
into Edinburgh for advice. There he died, and his sons,
interpreting his deepest wish and heedless of the expense,
brought him back all the thirteen miles of road, back
to his " lanely bield," whence on the morrow he was
taken up the trackless glen by the burnside on his
journey to the parish kirkyard—another four miles
away—and the whole countryside understood, and said
it was rightly done.

While James Thomson, the Weaver Poet of Currie,
was writing his verses, those of James Forrest, the
Weaver Poet of the Carlops, were finding publication in
the *Scots Magazine*.

Forrest was a self-taught follower of the Muse, born
in 1775, in the midst of the scenery of *The Gentle
Shepherd*. He laid no claim to genius—" with hand
unskilled, I touch the trembling lyre "—but his verses
are not without merit.—

" In rural solitude I pass my days
     Among the swains on Esk's fair winding stream ;
  To please myself I sing my artless lays ;
     To court the voice of fame I never dream."

Among others upon whom the literary spirit de-
scended were Sir James Ranken Fergusson of Spitalhaugh (*Poems and Ballads*, 1876) ; A. Farquharson, of
Lanely Bield, Carlops ; R. Sanderson of Linton (*Frae
the Lyne Valley*) ; William Welsh, a Peeblesshire cottar
(*Poetical and Prose Works*, 1856) ; and John Inglis,
shepherd in the Lyne Valley (*Poems and Songs*, 1866,

which includes " On Lyne Water," " Farewell to Wake-field on Lyne," and " Near Slipperfield ").

Allan Ramsay had no hesitation in selecting those to whom he would dedicate his Collection of Scots Proverbs—" the Farmers of the Dales and the Storemasters of the Hills." From his early days he knew the hill-side business. His pastoral comedy, *The Gentle Shepherd*, takes its action, thought, and colour from the Pentland Hills and Habbie's Howe, and the crofters, shepherds, milkmaids, and witches of the district. The attractive vividness of his descriptions could never have been attained but for his intimate acquaintance with the hills and his insight into Scottish rural life and character.

Is it to the poet Gay he would write—" the sonsy Gay," who caught the inspiration of the hills, and wrote *The Shepherd's Week* as well as *The Beggar's Opera*?—then he must think of him from the hills :

> " To thee, frae edge of Pentland height,
> Where fauns and fairies take delight,
> And revel a' the live-long night,
>   O'er glens and braes,
> A Bard that has the second sight
>   Thy fortune spaes."

Or is it to Thomson he is writing—him whose Nature poetry was to mark a new era in English literature ?— then he remembers that the genesis of *The Seasons* was under the shadow of Allermuir, where Mallet advised him to collect his scattered fragments and weave them into a single poem, while Mallet's own " William and Margaret " was composed on the banks of the Braid Burn, when he was a tutor at Dreghorn.

On one occasion, when writing to Forbes of Newhall, Ramsay praises the joy of youth, and begins :

> " Look up to Pentland's tow'ring tap,
>   Buried beneath great wreaths o' snaw,
> O'er ilka cleugh, ilk scar an' slap,
>   As high as ony Roman wa'."

Expressions such as " The Pentland Heights," " Pictland Hills," " Pentland's tow'ring tap," " Pictland Plains," and " We of Pictland " are found in his letters and poems.

Both Thomson and Gay knew the Pentlands through their patrons, who formed part of the literary coterie that gathered at Penicuik and Newhall in the early eighteenth century, many of whom were members of " The Worthy Club " that met in summer at Newhall as the guests of Sir David Forbes. Duncan Forbes of Culloden, Lord President of the Court of Session, one of the members, spent much of his leisure when Lord Advocate (1725) at the country seat of his cousin, John Forbes, who succeeded his father in Newhall, and here Ramsay had recited to his patrons and admirers the early version of his Pastoral Comedy before it was printed—a good, jovial, honest fellow who could "crack a bottle with the best," as Sir Walter Scott said in proposing the toast to his memory at the historic banquet in February 1827.

Thomson of *The Seasons* found in the Lord Advocate an early protector, and often accompanied him in his wanderings among the hills, enjoying those beauties of Nature which he has delineated with so high imagination and æsthetical delight.

William Aikman of Cairney, the portrait painter, also

befriended Thomson in London. He was a cousin of the Newhall laird; and his portraits of Thomson, Ramsay, and Gay are well known. Culloden was a welcome guest in London literary circles with Pope, Swift, Arbuthnot, and Gay; Henry Home (Lord Kames) owed much to his kindness and encouragement, and the scholarly Ruddiman, librarian of the Advocates' Library, also found in him a patron and friend.

The Duke and Duchess of Queensberry were patrons of the celebrated Gay, and the poet occasionally attended them on their excursions to Scotland. Gay certainly visited Ramsay at his shop in the Luckenbooths; and Tytler recollected Gay desiring Ramsay " to explain to him many of the Scottish expressions in the ' Pastoral Comedy,' which Gay said he would communicate to Pope," who was also interested.

Amidst all his activities in town, Ramsay never lost sight of his beloved hills and dales; they were interwoven with so many of his happiest moments and dearest recollections. The reason why he came to open his Comedy with a song to the tune " The Wauking o' the Faulds " is characteristic of his love for the pastoral scenes of rural husbandry and rustic simplicity. It was a July evening of great peace and beauty, and looking out from the House of Newhall to the verdant hill of Wester Spital, he saw on the sky-line the flock of the farm attended by the shepherd and his dog appearing from the other side of the hills, and gradually passing over and descending to the milking faulds and bughts above the House of Spital; the ewes to be milked there, as the custom was after the weaning of the lambs. A party was arranged to visit the scene next morning at sunrise. Ramsay's heart was thrilled at what he saw,

LANELY BIELD, HABBIE'S HOWE.

recalling his own boyhood—the early gathering of the ewes, with all its attendant sounds and picturesqueness, the milking in the bughts, the milkmaids and their pails, and the return of the flock and shepherds to the upland pastures—and with rapturous enthusiasm he exclaimed that in commemoration of what he had seen and enjoyed he would begin his Pastoral with " a sang to the tune ' The Wauking o' the Faulds ' " :

> " My Peggy sings sae saftly
> When on my pipe I play ;
> By a' the rest it is confes't
> By a' the rest that she sings best.
> My Peggy sings sae saftly
> And in her sangs are tauld
> With innocence, the wale o' sense,
> At wauking o' the fauld."

The original manuscript of *The Gentle Shepherd* is in Edinburgh University Library, and a copy of the Comedy presented to Burns by Allan Cunningham is in Edinburgh Public Library.

Chapter IX

CARLOPS—THE "GENTLE SHEPHERDS"

In the early years of last century Hansel Monday was one of the most exciting days of all the year in Carlops. The village was then a miniature "Thrums," with forty weavers, three grocers, three carriers, one tailor, two schoolmasters, two shoemakers, and four inns, and on the evening of that day the annual performance of Allan Ramsay's Pastoral Comedy, *The Gentle Shepherd*, was given by the local players:

> "To crowds at e'en, amidst the scenes
> That gave his drama birth,
> The Shepherds act it to the life,
> And crown his fame with mirth."

The homely language, characters, scenes, and nature of the play appealed to the villagers with a special appropriateness, and they eagerly learned their parts to the birr of the pirn and the song of the shuttle, for most of the younger members of the company were apprentice weavers. Few were the households that had not at least one young man who could recite long sections of it, and whose ambition was to act upon the stage the part of Roger or Patie, or even Jenny or Peggy, for girls were forbidden by the elders to take part in the play. The Hansel Monday performance held in the Carlops Mill was keenly anticipated by the players, and caused great excitement among the inhabitants of the countryside. The laird contributed towards the expenses, his object being to encourage the performance of the play in the district in which it was written, and to remove from the public mind the idea that Habbie's How was up the Glencorse Valley or that the play had any association with that district.

The opening scene depicts where Roger and Patie talk of their love affairs :

> " Beneath the south side of a craigy bield,
> Where crystal springs the halesome waters yield,
> Twa youthfu' shepherds on the gowans lay,
> Tenting their flocks ae bonny morn of May,"

and where Peggy and Jenny introduce a like discussion at the washing green behind Newhall :

> JEN. Come, Meg, let's fa' to wark upon this green,
> The shining day will bleach our linen clean ;
> The waters clear, the lift unclouded blue,
> Will make them like a lily wet with dew.

> PEG. Gae far'er up the burn to Habbie's How,
> Where a' the sweets of spring and simmer grow ;
> Between twa birks, out o'er a little lin,
> The water fa's and maks a singand din ;
> A pool breast-deep, beneath as clear as glass,
> Kisses, with easy whirls, the bordering grass.
> We'll end our washing while the morning's cool,
> And when the day grows het, we'll to the pool,
> There wash oursels—'tis healthfu' now in May,
> And sweetly cauler on sae warm a day.

JEN.   Daft lassie, when we're naked, what'll ye say,
  Gif our twa herds come brattling down the brae,
  And see us sae ? that jeering fallow Pate
  Wad taunting say, Haith, lasses ye're no blate.

PEG.   We're far frae ony road, and out of sight ;
  The lads they're feeding far beyont the height.
  But tell me now, dear Jenny (we're our lane),
  What gars ye plague your wooer with disdain ?

The Carlops players also visited the surrounding districts. A barn would be fitted up, staging, lighting, and seating accommodation were of the most primitive kind, but " the play's the thing," and two performances running into the early hours of the morning were not uncommon.

The story is told that on one occasion at Penicuik, when in the course of the play " Sir William " is recognized by Mause and the others, the audience were so pleased that their applause became uproarious, in the midst of which one end of a form gave way, and a score of lads and lasses were precipitated on to the floor, but after waiting for a minute or two " to let the dirdum blaw ower," the players went on to finish the play.

They also visited Peebles, but it was with some trepidation that the Carlops Company ventured there, for the Peebles folks had had a taste of play-acting some years previously by the French prisoners who were located there, and while the Carlops Company had been very successful in Penicuik, still, it was argued, it " wasna to be expected that the folk of Penicuik were unco' great judges of play-acting when a' they had ever seen in that line was ' Punch and Judy ' at the Fairs." So off the Company set—fourteen in number—one fine frosty morning in January, to play *The Gentle Shepherd*

in Peebles.   There were no motor-buses in those days !
A horse and cart were provided, the horse " decked out
with ribbons, and Geordie Soutar sitting on the foreside,
fiddlin', and the rest of the company a' as merry as mice
in a mouldy cheese, with the Carlops folk a' at their
doors seeing them off "—so wrote a contemporary.
Even the hens thrawed their heads sideways, and stood
on one leg, while the cocks glowered first with one fixed
eye, then with the other, arched their necks disdain-
fully, and wondered in a haughty fashion what all the
stir was about.

It was a great occasion, and there was no anti-climax
when Peebles was reached, and the play proceeded.   It
was a triumph all the way.   The hall—a ballroom—
was crowded, chairs for the more important of the
townsfolk, such as bailies and magistrates, and seats
for ordinary folk at threepence and sixpence each, unless
there happened to be a big family, when an inclusive
charge was made.   Thirty candles supplied the foot-
lights, two doorkeepers collected the cash, Geordie
Soutar played the fiddle between the acts to keep the
audience from wearying, and tailor Sharpshears of the
Carlops acted as Prompter.

Amusing incidents were not infrequent.   " Glaud,"
the old Shepherd, was dressed in a blue coat with brass
buttons and high collar, blue knee-breeches, rig-and-fur
stockings and shoes with brass buckles, and long white
hair from a cow's tail hanging down over his haffits.   In
his " muckle braid blue bonnet," which he declared was
big enough to hold a peck o' tatties, he had stuffed some
straw in order to protect half a dozen eggs which he had
received as a present earlier in the evening.   In his
excitement he walked on to the stage without his bonnet,

and then suddenly realizing that his bonnet was wanting, he returned to the dressing-room, placed it upon his head, and then, rushing back to the platform, gave it a pull to make it sit rightly, when, alas, the golden stream of yellow yolks flowed down over his brow and nose and chin, and over his cow's-tail locks and blue coat. This was greeted with loud applause as being part of the play.

Another character, " Bauldy," was also the source of much amusement. In the course of the Wedding Feast a haggis was brought in, but Bauldy fumbled in the handling of it in taking it from the attendant, and over-balanced the platter, and the steaming haggis toppled over on to Glaud's lap. Glaud got such a fright that the chair upon which he sat was upset, and Glaud and the chair and the haggis rolled together on the boards. This roused the audience to intense excitement, rising to their feet and applauding vociferously, unaware of the condition of the three victims—the " Chieftain o' the Puddin' Race " wi' a broken croon, the chair wi' a broken back, and Glaud—whose sweetheart sat in the front row—wi' a broken heart !

In another scene where " Madge " strikes " Bauldy," and he retires with his nose bleeding, the effect of this was produced with bright red paint smeared on a cloth ; but Bauldy picked up the wrong " cloot," and as he left the stage amidst great laughter, he was horrified to find that his nose and face had been daubed with blue.

When the weaving industry declined, the Carlops Club of Players became less flourishing, but the play, with its humour and insight into rustic manners and customs, was a great favourite in all the countryside for many a day.

The Prologue—considered by the local inhabitants as being quite as important as the play itself—was written specially for each occasion, and the following specimen, which was composed by James Forrest, was recited for the first time at a performance at Rogers-rig in 1807 :

" Here are no foreign actors with laced coats,
  Who ne'er can speak a word o' plain braid Scots,
  But simple country folks, who seek no fame ;
  Just to amuse you is our greatest aim.
  Have patience then a while, till I rehearse
  My Prologue short, in rough, unpolished verse—

  Thanks be to Allan, that queer, funny wight,
  Who wrote the play we mean to act this night.
  What though it lash some follies o' the age ;
  Fair virtue shines triumphant in each page :
  Here's steady loyalty, that nought could move ;
  Friendship sincere ; and truth ; and constant love ;
  Beauty in tears while hope eludes her view,
  Fair like the lily wet with vernal dew.

  Such were the lays blythe Ramsay sweetly sung,
  When on the banks of Esk his lyre was strung ;
  As oft he wooed the Muse at twilight's fall
  Among the greenwood glades around Newhall.
  So long as May produces smelling flowers ;
  So long as bees delight in sunny hours ;
  So long as truth with innocence shall dwell ;
  So long THE GENTLE SHEPHERD shall excel.
  Let bigots rail ; and kankart critics snarl ;
  And crafty priests about sma' matters quarrel ;
  We scorn alike their malice and their rage ;
  There's nought immoral seen upon our stage."

Chapter X

JAMES THOMSON, THE WEAVER POET

In a romantic spot above Currie village, and under the heathery heights of the Pentland Hills, lived James Thomson, the Weaver Poet. From the door of his cottage, which he named " Parnassus," there was to the north an uninterrupted view of the Highland hills, Fife, and the Firth of Forth, while near by a Pentland burn that rises in the Maidenscleugh runs to join the Water of Leith between steep banks, tree clad, and flower bedecked. This glen, which is not difficult of access, with its lovers' walk and rustic bridge, is still known as the Poet's Glen, and the Bard's Bower and Well are there, with the following verse by the poet inscribed above the latter :

" My water's refreshing and perhaps may inspire
The enraptured mind with poetical fire ;
I'm as wholesome and free to all who here passes,
As the Fount from the side of the Grecian Parnassus.
    —Jamie Thamson's Helicon."

He had many favourite retreats where, when his day's work was done, he sought the silence of the hills or the musical murmur of the Kenleith Burn to sooth the cares of his anxious life in reveries of fancy.

From the collection of his poems in the Scottish

NORTH ESK VALLEY NEAR MARFIELD.

dialect, published in 1801, we learn that Thomson was " nursed in obscurity and never shared the caresses of a father nor experienced the fondness of a mother." He was brought up by his grandparents in Currie, who taught him to read and to understand.

As he herded his grandfather's cow he eagerly devoured a book of ballads and songs, and thus acquired a taste for poetry. Allan Ramsay's poems were his chief delight, and *The Gentle Shepherd* he learned to repeat from beginning to end, while in the evenings neighbour herds would gather round their new-found prodigy of learning and listen to his songs and entertaining rhymes.

At the age of thirteen he became apprenticed as a weaver to his grandfather, not of choice, for it is said that he had higher aspirations, but of necessity. " Poverty had marked him for her own, and the visionary schemes of youthful ardour yielded to the voice of imperious necessity."

When the work of the day was over he went to school, and learned to write, his great delight being to make rhymes on his schoolfellows. " Willie Weir's Legacy," containing twenty-five verses,

> " O' the utensils, gudes, an' gear,
> That did belong to Willie Weir,"

was one of his earliest pieces.

Out of his savings he bought a fiddle, and the poet became musician, and diffused music and festivity wherever he went.

He resided for a time in Colinton, where, in 1787, he married a Currie lass, and had a family of seven daughters and one son. In this connection his fiddle came in useful :

> " I gie my bairnies a' a tune
>   To keep them cheery,
> An' gar them dance, without their shoon,
>   Till they be weary."

Later he returned to Kenleith, where he continued
as a country weaver. The inspiration he had received
in his early days as a herd boy, when he led the simple
pastoral life under the shelter of the Pentland Hills,
remained with him all his days. The beauty he saw in
Nature he strove to put into verse ; she was his guide
and monitress, while " the excellent Ramsay " and " the
still more excellent Fergusson " were his heroes ; and
so he sang.

The *Historical Magazine* of 1799 refers to the discovery
of a second Burns " possessed of no small portion of
poetic fire, who, though constantly engaged from morning till night in the laborious employment of a common
country weaver, still finds leisure to cultivate the Muse,
even though borne down by the iron hand of poverty.
. . . He is universally esteemed and considered as a
sober, industrious, well-behaved man." It also quotes
one of his poems—" The Ghaist."

Sometimes he wrote out his verses, and these were
handed round among the neighbouring farmers, and by
this means the weaver's claims as a poet came to the
notice of the Currie minister. Not that Thomson was
unknown to the minister ; on the contrary, he was the
most useful man in the parish. Besides being a weaver
and a musician, he became physician to the village—he
could let blood when the neighbours required his aid ;
kill a mart for the accommodation of a friend ; and on
Saturday night all the beards of the village came under
his hand, and when the minister's razors required an

edge they were sent to Jamie Thamson, and duly returned to the minister with a few humorous verses appropriate to the occasion.

In due time his poems came to circulate among the good minister's friends, and his admirers increased, so that when the time arrived for their publication the list of subscribers totalled over six hundred. The list is included at the end of the book, and among the names are such as His Grace the Duke of Buccleuch, Principal Baird of the University, Lord Cullen, Lady Dundas, etc. The names of seventy-five " chiels o' law " are included, who are referred to in the " Poet's Address to his Book," in his own humorous way, as " warst o' a' the three ! " He seemed to delight in poking fun at the lawyers. A second edition was published at Leith in 1819 and a new edition, edited by R. B. Langwill, in 1894. Ghosts and witches were not unknown in Currie ; indeed, in former days Currie was at one time notorious for its practisers of " the black art," and several of Thomson's poems deal with this subject.

A certain gentleman's seat in the parish was believed to be haunted. A lady in white had been seen gliding through the woods in the silence of the night ; strange sounds were heard when the bird of night sits plaining to the moon ; and indescribable phantoms had appeared to lonely travellers as they journeyed along. In " The Ghaist " he tells the story of this lady in white.

In his descriptive poetry, with its simple and natural language, he faithfully depicts the beauties of Nature around him and the simple manners of the sons of toil. His forte seems to have been in the expression of genuine human feeling and love of Nature.

Chapter XI

CAMPS, CAIRNS, AND CIRCLES

FROM the inspiration of the hills, by which those who dwelt among them were moved to serve the Muses, we turn to consider some of the mysterious things that are to be found there by those who go in search of them ; and since no one can foretell what discoveries may yet be made, in view of the wonderful revelations recently made by Professor Gordon Childe at Castlelaw, the subject appeals to the imagination more strongly now than ever before.

In the Royal Commission's Report on the " Ancient and Historical Monuments and Constructions" in Midlothian, we learn that the slopes of the Pentlands, although untouched by the plough, have yielded comparatively few signs of ancient human habitation. The signs may be wanting, but we may assume that " ancient constructions " must have been made by ancient peoples.

Of the cairns on the hilltops, for instance, we are told that presumably they belong to the Bronze Age. Genuine " hilltop " cairns are found on Carnethy and on the East Cairn Hill. On Caerketton there are some scattered remains of a cairn, and it is to be deplored that the stones from this cairn have evidently been used in the building of the adjoining dyke. All that remains of the cairn is a collection of small stones, fifty-three feet in diameter and five feet in height.

The cairn on Carnethy, the second highest hill in the Pentlands, is seventy feet in diameter and eight feet in height, and the stones are of small size. In this case also it is unfortunate that the cairn has been disturbed by the building of small cairns upon it, but, the Report continues, " apparently the core has not been opened."

Although the cairn on the East Cairn Hill is smaller than the Carnethy cairn, being only fifty-five feet in diameter and six to eight feet in height, it is much more interesting in that some of the stones are of considerable size, and apart from the Surveyors' Cairn upon it, this fine circular cairn has not been disturbed. The stones appear to have come from the immediate vicinity.

The Pentland Walker naturally asks himself how these cairns came to be there. They did not arrive on the hill-top by accident or natural evolution ; some one must have brought them there. One theory is that on the highest hills, and frequently on hills within sight of one another, the Druids, who worshipped the sun as the " source of all things," worshipped on the hilltops. There also fires were kindled and sacrifice offered in honour of the sun, whose genial warmth in springtime was welcomed and recognized in their Whitsunday festival. The harvest of the fruits of the earth was honoured in the Hallow-eve festival. Every worshipper carried a stone, and added it to the cairn. Many antiquarians now say there never were such people as the Druids, although several writers of antiquity, including Julius Cæsar, have contributed to our knowledge of the mysterious Order.

It is interesting to note that the ancient name of the East Cairn Hill was the "Harpers' Hill," from the Bards, who were of the Order of the Druids, and used the harp as an accompaniment to their songs—an instrument that was also used by the bards of the Britons, Caledonian Picts, and Scots.

The mysterious Druids are also supposed to have had something to do with the stone circles, and of such there was at one time a specimen near Marchwell Farm. Unfortunately, when the Edinburgh–Biggar road was being made, it cut through the knoll north-east of the farm upon which the circle was formed, and only two of the seven stones—about fifteen inches above the ground—remain in their original position, the other five being in close proximity. They are of a basaltic character, and appear to have been brought from a distance. A note to Dr. Pennecuik's *Panegyrick upon the Royal Army in Scotland, 1685*, published in 1715, states that " the site of the camp of General Thomas Dalziel of Binns at Rullion Green is marked by a ring of gray whinstones, near the House o' Muir, southward from it, and is still shown to the peasantry, who report him to have been a warlock or wizard."

By some antiquarians such circles are thought to have been temples or courts of justice, the Druids being judges as well as priests. In this connection we may note that at Carlops, east of the Brig, between the main road and Roger's Rig Farm, there is an eminence called the Girt or Girth Hill, and the Girths, we are informed in Tolland's *History of the Druids*, were judicial circles, in the vicinity of their temples. A tradition regarding them in some parts of the country is that the people resorted to them for justice, and that they served nearly the same purpose among the Celts as the cities of refuge did among the Jews. In the reigns of James III. and James IV. they were resorted to as sanctuaries, and the name still survives in such place-names as Auldgirth, Tundergirth, and Girthland in the south of Scotland.

Not only is there this ancient relic of pagan days at Marchwell, but on the east slope of Lawhead Hill in the immediate vicinity, about five hundred yards from Lawhead Fort—to which we shall presently refer—to the south of a belt of trees, in rough ground, there are seven earthen circles, five forming an irregular line from north-east to south-west, and two lying a short distance to the east. The most northerly circle is the best preserved, the central area being nine feet in diameter, and surrounded by a low bank six feet broad with a shallow trench four feet broad outside, the diameter over all being twenty-nine feet. The bank is less noticeable in the other examples; four of them have over all an average diameter of twenty-eight feet.

Still another circle on the eastern slopes of the Pentlands, unlike any of the foregoing, falls to be mentioned. In the Commission's Report it is described as a " circular construction " and is situated on the summit of Dod Rig, above Spital Farm, Ninemileburn. Most Pentland Walkers have regarded this circular enclosure as merely a large sheep stell, such as is frequently found in high and hilly pasture land, but the plan and masonry show that the structure originally served a different purpose. The outer wall of the enclosure, built of rubble and mortar, is three feet four inches thick, and has been raised to five feet and repaired in dry-stone dyking. There are two compartments of unequal size, the dividing wall stopping short of the encircling wall

at each end, giving communication at these points
between the two divisions. On the north side of the
partition is an entrance in the outer wall.

It is not known to what period such walled enclosures
belong, but it is thought that they are probably of
later date than the forts, and may have been home-
steads, or possibly "birrens" used for the concealment
of stock.

In the present case it may be remembered that the
district is said to have belonged to the monastery of
Newhall, which had also two other buildings under its
care known as the Fore 'Spital, on the site of Spital
Farm, and the Back 'Spital, on the other side of the hill
on the banks of the infant Esk, and that these buildings
may have existed and served their purpose as hospitals
for the care of the sick and the superannuated, and as
inns for travellers, for the convents were the only inns
in those days.

And as there was on the ridge a track over the Monks'
Rig with a cross, set in a socket which may still be seen,
and doubtless serving the double purpose of a wayside
shrine and a mark of direction for travelling monks going
over the hills to Queensferry, we may conclude that the
" circular construction " may have formed part of the
Fore 'Spital, and been used as a place of safety from the
wild animals, which we know roamed the hills in those
early centuries. The Fore 'Spital remained undissolved
until the Reformation in 1560, and was modernized about
1750.

The Pentland Walker will also visit the fine specimen
of a cup-and-ring marked stone which now finds a resting-
place at Glencorse Parish Church, having recently been
removed from the wood adjoining the Old Kirk. The

EARTH HOUSE, CASTLELAW FORT.

HUNTERS' TRYST.

boulder is of red sandstone, and bears traces of glacial striation ; it is three feet in length, and is covered with a group of cup-and-ring markings, connected in some instances by clearly defined gutters. Where it came from originally, by whom it was sculptured, and what is the significance of the markings we do not know. Other specimens were found on the Blackford Hill in 1926, and on the Braid Hills Golf Course in 1897, and these are now in the National Museum of Antiquities.

Perhaps the most interesting of all the relics of ancient days to be found on the hills are the camps or " forts." Of these there are four along the south-eastern slopes— at Hillend, Castlelaw, Lawhead, and Camp Hill, Braidwood—all situated at or over 1,000 feet above sea-level.

Of Hillend Fort, behind an old quarry, on the crest of a small spur jutting out from the base of Caerketton, only a few traces remain, the details being completely destroyed. A short section shows that there had been at least two lines of defence, and a row of fairly large stones set edge to edge for 35 feet indicates that the defences were in part of stone. The area is approximately 200 feet in diameter.

Castlelaw, 200 yards north of the farm of that name, and Lawhead, 700 yards north-west of Lawhead farm, commanding a view of each other across the intervening Glencorse valley, 1¼ miles between, are both oval in plan, with an internal measurement of 270 feet by 120 feet, and 285 feet by 182 feet respectively, and are surrounded by ramparts and ditches. Castlelaw has three lines of defence and three entrances. In the case of Lawhead the defences are well defined on the north-west segment, where there is rough ground, but the remainder of the construction lies in a grass field and is now obliterated. There are two entrances, and inside the fort are three circular enclosures.

The fort on Camp Hill, about 400 yards north-west of Braidwood Bridge, Eightmileburn, is a well-defined hill fort, also oval in shape and measuring internally 232 feet by 175 feet. The defences comprise an inner ditch, a rampart of stone and earth, and an outer ditch, and the fort has three entrances. In the centre are indications of some circular and oval structures, which differ from the usual hut structure in having a slight mound surrounded by a ditch instead of a hollow surrounded by remains of a wall. Similar constructions are found in both Lawhead and Castlelaw, which makes them specially interesting. These forts, along with that at Clubbiedean, on the north-western slope, are described in detail in the Commission's Report, in which they are referred to as " defensive constructions."

As to the date, the purpose and the inhabitants of these forts, we have, until recently, had no definite knowledge, although it was generally accepted that they were habitations of the early Britons, hill villages situated above the marshy ground, with defences, not necessarily against organized forces, but against roving bands or tribes, or against the wild animals that roamed the hills.

In the summer of 1931 and 1932 Castlelaw Fort, situated 500 feet above the Glencorse Burn, was opened up and examined under the direction of Professor Gordon Childe. One explanation of these little camps is that they were used for defence by the native tribes when rumours of Agricola's warlike preparations reached them ; and Castlelaw may be regarded as typical of such forts in North Britain. It is not a hilltop town, like the English forts, and it was abandoned as a fort before the close of the Roman period in Caledonia. But what makes Castlelaw Fort unique, south of the Forth, is that when defence was no longer required an earth house was built inside the old camp—an underground retreat, a beehive chamber, eleven feet in diameter. It was cut in the rock, with walls faced with dry masonry composed of boulders brought up from the valley below, and in it men lived, at least in times of punitive expeditions or of inclement weather. The earth house, then, is of later date than the fort. The relics found in the earth house prove it to have been in occupation *during the second century*, and probably prior to the abandonment of the Antonine Vallum about A.D. 180, the second phase of close contact between Roman and native.

On the rough rock floor were found " gnawed bones, bits of cheap pots imported from Gaul, Roman glass, and ornaments in native style, but made in Germany ; a little iron was smelted and slag was left lying about. The irregular rock floor was, at a later date, covered with clean clay, and Roman glass was splintered on the relaid floor ; an unfinished spindle whorl, dropped by a woman, lay in the passage, and a stag's antler was stuck in a cranny of the wall."

All the excavations were planned and photographed, and then reburied. Some day they will be made accessible to inspection. When further excavations have been made in this and the other forts, fuller information may be forthcoming. Meantime the ancient cairns, stone and earthen circles, " circular constructions," cup-and-ring marked stones, and " forts " still excite the Hill-walker's curiosity and imagination, because they record, in mute monuments of earth and stone, the faith in strange oracles and the fight for existence of the ancient inhabitants of our wonderful Hills of Home.

Chapter XII

COMMONTIES, MARKETS, AND INNS

HILL-WALKERS and trampers are exploring Scotland to-day as never before. Their desire is to get off the main roads, and to find out and traverse the old cross-country tracks and drove roads, and in this the Scottish Rights-of-Way Society is doing a great amount of quiet and effective work by recovering and preserving for the public, rights-of-way all over the country which would otherwise fall into desuetude. This Society deserves the support of all Pentland Walkers.

The various approaches to the Pentland Hills were not always hedged round with private lands and forbidden paths. At many points there were " commonties," or commons, for the pasturage of sheep and cattle, by which there was free access to the hills. One of those was " the Commonty of Pentland Hills," which extended from Colinton to Hillend ; hence the field-path rights-of-way which we enjoy to-day by Dreghorn, Oxgangs, and Comiston, and which in other days were " roads to the Common." Commons began to disappear after the Act of 1695, which authorized the division of such lands among the neighbouring proprietors under a Court of Session process. Many of these " cases " were long drawn out. Law agents were instructed, commissioners were appointed, witnesses were interrogated, doubtful dividing lines were discussed, the bounds of the Commonty were perambulated by all interested, rights-of-way were settled, and irascible landlords pacified by the wise counsel of the judge upon the necessity of a little give-and-take if the heritors' boundaries were to be adjusted and regulated for the advantage of all in general. Then last of all the march stones were set up.

The Commonty of Pentland Hills was divided among the heritors in 1709, each proprietor getting land for the pasturage of so many score of sheep in proportion to the value of his estate. The estates and parties interested were: Colinton—Sir James Foulis; Woodhall —Sir William Fowlis; Dreghorn—Patrick Pitcairne; Swanston and Bowbridge—John Trotter, of Mortonhall; Colmistoun (Comiston)—Sir Walter Porterfield; Swanston — Henry Hamilton; Reidhall — Alexander Brand, of Castlebrand; and the Temple lands of Swanston—Duncan and Alison Robertson. The whole area pastured 330 score of sheep (ten sheep to the score).

Much interesting evidence was submitted, and many of the place-names used at that time in delimiting the boundaries have now disappeared. Capelaw at the head of the Howden Glen (Howdoun Head) was adjudged part of the Commonty because of evidence that sheep and cattle were formerly pastured there in summer time, and brought down at harvest time. One witness deponed that " he had known the oxen of Swanston, and the oxen and sheep of Comiston, and the staigs of the Temple lands of Swanston, pasture upon that hill ever since the Battle of Rullion Green " in 1666. The farm of Leeps, in Boghall valley, of which only a few

juniper bushes and nettles now remain to mark the site,
did not fall within the Commonty, the boundary line
being stated as the Wildmuir or Sweep Road " amongst
the marches betwixt Swanston and the Leeps," and as
proving that Leeps lay outside the boundary a witness
deponed that in 1651 he " hounded the gear off the
Leeps " when they strayed below the Wildmuir Road.

Pitcairne of Dreghorn protested vigorously against the
passage through his ground—the Loan of Dreghorn—
being awarded as a right-of-way to the possessor and
tenants of the west part of the Barony of Colinton and
Mains of Reidhall, but Lord Bowhill, the presiding
judge, said there was no ground for the protestation,
and that the said passage to the Lord Colinton and Reidhall and their tenants should be " through the Loan and
through the Commonty." In the discussion Pitcairne
objected, alleging that a servitude could not be introduced upon his property without his consent, whereby
his corns and grass would be prejudiced and tenants
discouraged to take lands burdened with such a servitude and common passage going straight by the gates
of his house. But it was answered for the other heritors
that Mr. Pitcairne's prejudice was " imaginary and
affected " ; that in all divisions of commonty it was
necessary that alterations be made of former possession
without which the process could never take effect to the
advantage of all parties concerned, and that it would
prove very burdensome and inconvenient if the passage
from the several heritors' grounds was not to be adjusted
and regulated to the advantage of all in general.

Pitcairne denied that the Loan was ever a common
passage, and " when the same was attempted their goods
were stopped and interrupted, which Dreghorn can

prove and make appear." He was determined not to
allow the passage to be a common loan, but the Lords
resolved otherwise.

Subsequent proprietors also endeavoured to defy the
Court and to close this road, and one of them fixed
gates across it, but this was met by the inhabitants
commissioning a horseman to ride through the Loan
and over the path through Howden Glen annually to
preserve the right-of-way.

The Court also granted passage to the tenants of
Comiston and the Lord Colinton's tenants of their
" Maynes and Oxgangs " through Mortonhall's grounds
—hence the road by Colinton Mains Farm, the path by
Oxgangs, and the road to the hills by Comiston Farm to
Swanston, formerly called the " Common Loan to the
Commonty."

The Temple lands of Swanston were of small extent.
In presenting to the Court the claim of the proprietors,
Sir James Grant, advocate, stated there was no valua-
tion of the lands, being Temple lands, and thereby
" paying nothing to Croon nor Kirk." He produced
three consecutive tacks showing a yearly payment of
£20, with six hens or 40 shillings and the carriage of
two loads of coal from Loanhead. He therefore claimed
for a proportionate part of the Commonty. The lands
were accordingly valued at £4, 3s. 4d., entitling the
owners to land for half a score of sheep.

At one time Swanston had a larger population than
Colinton, but the early history, if there is any, is difficult
to find. It was Swan's town, but we do not know who
Swan was. We know that the Templars possessed a
small part of the lands, and part was also associated with
the monks of Whitekirk as a grange or resting-place.

"WINTER LINGERS IN THE LAP OF SPRING."

The Glencorse Commonty was divided in 1795. It lay between Greenlaw House and Rullion Green. Greenlaw is mentioned in the Woodhouselee MSS. in connection with Prince Charlie's Highlanders in 1745, and the prison into which the mansion house was converted was used as the first of its kind in Scotland for prisoners in the wars with Napoleon. The site is now occupied by Glencorse Barracks, the depot of the Royal Scots Regiment.

In 1612 the magistrates of Edinburgh gave to Lord Abernethy of Salton the superiority of the three husband-lands of Salton in exchange for the right of holding fairs at the House of Muir, and the sheep markets there continued in existence for over two hundred and fifty years, half of the market dues being paid to the city and the other half to the chief heritor, the Laird of Glencorse.

Where there was a market there was also an inn, for to this market sheep were brought from far distances, those from the north crossing the Forth at Queensferry, and travelling over the drove roads converging upon the old road which can still be traced on the south side of Glencorse Reservoir, opposite the Kirk Burn, leading to the village of Turnhouse and the market-place. The inn is now the farmhouse of Marchwell, above Flotterstane, on the Edinburgh–Biggar highway. Here surely was " The Shepherds' Tryst," if near by there was also a " Fishers' Tryst " and a " Hunters' Tryst."

We read of Marchwell Inn in the year of the Commonty division. From the account of expenses incurred in the process, which lasted for five years, we find that a " Coach hyre " from Edinburgh to House of Muir, with the commissioner " to perambulat the Commonty," cost

£1, 8s., of which 3s. to the driver ; and the " Paid Bill in Hunter's Tavern (Mrs. Hunter was the proprietrix of the inn) on return from perambulating the Commonty " amounted to £5, with a further 1s. 8½d. " for a sheet of stamped paper for writing certain Depositions, and incidents, in the Coffee House "—presumably the tavern.

Legal deeds and documents are not infrequently put away in such sure and certain places that when necessity arises they cannot be found. So it was in the case of the Glencorse Commonty Division, for we find that in 1795 a fee of a guinea was " paid to the Keeper of the General Register House for their trouble making a search for the Warrants of a Process of Souming and Rouming of the Commonty previous to the beginning of this century, which they could not find." " Souming " and " Rouming," it may be explained, are two old words signifying the form of law by which the number of cattle that each proprietor may pasture upon the moor is ascertained.

A fee of 2s. 6d. had been paid to a clerk five years before—1790—to look out " the former Summons of Division of the Commonty," but it had not been forthcoming, and in 1795 we find 1s. 4d. paid to the surveyor for making a copy of " Decerniture of the Decreet of Souming and Rouming of the Commonty in 1661 as to the proportion of the Heritors," and 8s. for making a plan of the Commonty.

However, after the bounds had been " perambulat " and the division made, all adjourned to Hunter's Tavern to meet with the commissioner and the agents for the heritors, and the bill to celebrate the conclusion of the case amounted to £9 ! The commissioner got twenty guineas " for his trouble," his clerks two guineas, and the mason, " for quarrying, hewing, and lettering March Stones set up to divide the Commonty," £2, 15s. 6d.

But there was still another item of expense, and it finds a place at the end of the account. We need not be surprised that the Keeper of the General Register House could not find the " Decreet of Souming and Rouming." It was not there. It was in Penicuik, and so we find that another lawyer was paid four guineas " for his trouble in going to Pennycuick to look for the Decreet, dated 31st July 1691, and for making a Notarial Copy thereof—20 sheets." Altogether the expense of the process amounted to over £150, which was paid proportionately by the City of Edinburgh, Clerk of Penicuik, Bothwell of Glencorse, and Caddel of Greenlaw.

The House of Muir markets were closed in 1871. One who visited the markets tells me that those held on the first and second Mondays of April were largely attended, and presented a busy scene in the picturesque setting among the hills of Castlelaw, Turnhouse, and Carnethy. Drovers, shepherds, sheep, and dogs were on the way from all parts of the country making for the " Hoose o' Mair " for weeks before the markets.

Great preparations required to be made at the inn for the feeding and housing of so many hungry drovers, buyers and sellers, farmers and butchers, herds and orramen. Carriers' carts were heavily laden with merchandise, including farm implements, and accessories in iron, wood, and earthenware, and stores of provisions, while to the back of the cart were affixed crates for the carriage of fowls. There are two steep gradients in the road from Flotterstane Brig to " Merchwell," and trace

horses were required for the carts. The carrier's dog
chained to the axle seemed to know what was required of
him also, and pulled as eagerly as the horses. The lads
in charge of the tracers, supplied by the neighbouring
farmers, had a great day of it, and were well pleased
with a copper or two for their fee.

The inn was a short distance from the market-place,
and business was brisk at the fair, so Mrs. Hunter, the
proprietrix, had two tents erected in the field, where
she dispensed whisky, beer and porter, pies, sandwiches,
and gingerbread, and at the end of the day carried back
her drawings, mostly in copper, in a clothes-basket.
Many a bargain was settled in the inn, and after the
buying and selling at the markets had ceased most of
the dealers adjourned to Mrs. Hunter's, where the story
of the day's bargains and prices was told and retold.
And on Saturday nights, when neighbour bodies met,
there was many a jollification and joke. " Times were
better then," said my friend, " folks were happier an'
better off, there was mair fun an' frolic, and nae herm
in it, and eh, man, what nichts we had wi' the fiddle ! "

The story is told of a shepherd, in the employment of
a neighbouring laird, who was noted for his bushy, silky
beard, that kept him warm on many a winter night
when his jacket was buttoned over it. During the
evening in the inn, one half of the beard was cut off,
all unknown to the shepherd. He arrived home somewhat late, or early, and after replying to the inquiries of
his goodwife that he had been to " Merchwell," and that
he was well and happy, he crept into bed, still uncon-
scious of his loss. But the consternation of his spouse
in the morning when she saw her husband can better be
imagined than described ; many a laugh the " ferm

hands " had over it, and it became a standing joke in the countryside how Sandy lost his beard.

The inn at Marchwell was not the only one that received the patronage of the ferm chiels and other callants. The Fishers' Tryst at Milton Bridge was another. Colonel Trotter of Bush had in his employment one who was a character in the countryside, who told many a joke and played many a prank.

He was a cronie at the Fishers' Tryst, and one Saturday night was merrier than usual. On the way home after eleven o'clock he had to pass the Old Kirk at Glencorse, and the story goes that on the way he found a white goat wandering about. Charlie got hold of the goat, and had an idea. Pulling the goat after him to the kirk, he tied the bell-rope to the animal's horns, and made off across the countryside for home.

Meanwhile the bell began to ring, and as the goat danced about, the bell went on clanging in a different fashion from its wont, till all the parish was wide awake and wondering what could be the reason at such an hour. Some of the inhabitants ventured forth to find out. The first to arrive proceeded cautiously till, in the darkness, he espied through the trees a white form with horns dancing about the kirk door, when, throwing up his arms in horrified alarm, he cried out, " It's the de'il himsel', it's the de'il himsel', ringin' the bell ! "

In due course the wonted silence of the parish was restored, but tongues continued to wag about " the de'il pu'in' the bell o' Torrence's kirk."

Charlie was an orraman, and longed at times for other employment. The post of gravedigger, beadle, and general attendant at the Glencorse Kirk fell vacant, and he thought this would be a fine post for him. So one morning he approached the Colonel, the chief heritor, who was to interview applicants.

" What's up to-day ? " said the Colonel.

" Well, sir," said Charlie, " I'm wantin' a constant job ; dae ye think I'll hae ony chance o' the grave-diggin' job ? "

" Grave-diggin', grave-diggin'," said the Colonel, " a constant job, a constant job—do you want to bury a' the folk in the parish ? "

Poor Charlie didn't get the job.

The tales told at the inn were many and various. The Rev. William Torrence, the old minister of Glencorse, was a man of small stature, and used to stand upon a stool in the pulpit. On one of his last appearances there, and preaching from the text, " A little while and ye shall see Me no more," he became so moved with his subject that he stumbled off the stool and disappeared, so fulfilling literally the words of his text and affording much ill-timed amusement to his flock.

His son Alexander, who succeeded him, was fond of curling, and entertained the local club annually at Fishers' Tryst. On one occasion, among his morning service intimations he gave out that there would be no service in the church that evening, but that " they would meet at the curling pond to-morrow morning at eleven o'clock."

The dry humour of a local worthy is seen in his comment made to the good minister's recommendation of the dram he was giving him. " Yes, it is over a hundred years old," said the minister. " Aye, aye, an' ye tell me so, yes, yes—well it hasna grown verra much ! "

Chapter XIII

THE OLD KIRK OF GLENCORSE

In the days of summer the old Kirk of Glencorse is a kind of Mecca for wayfarers, tourists, and pilgrims from near at hand and far away. What is the magnet that attracts so many? Is it the ruin of the prehistoric place of worship in the valley with its ancient graves, and cup-marked stone that was at one time set upon an adjacent knoll, surrounded with the magic tracery of exquisite woodland scenery, through cunning vistas of which peep the Pentland peaks? Or is it an interest in the " pathetic " tombstones, the epitaphs, the coats-of-arms—of the Purveses of Woodhouselee, Bothwells of Glencorse, Campbells of Armaddie? Can it be the stories of the Spanish princess who died in despair for her lover, languishing in the Greenlaw prison hard by, or of the French prisoners of war who settled their quarrels in fights with scissor-blades; or the memory of the Torrence family, father and son, who ministered there in holy things for over a hundred years?

Or is it that the spirit of Stevenson haunts the spot? Can it be that his works are now so universally read and the fame of their author so gone to the ends of the earth that tourists must now visit the place where the literary artist playfully suggested that his spirit might wander? Probably it is the Stevenson story that is the magnet.

His letters about Glencorse to Colvin and to Crockett, written from the South Seas, are known to most, while his poem of the Hills of Home, the Martyrs of the Covenant, and the haunting call of the peeweets, contains mystic utterances that appeal to all susceptible natures, wise and simple alike. His few references to the old kirk and the old minister have so fixed themselves upon the imagination of Stevenson worshippers that his words have now attained an importance which their author little anticipated.

It is not unlikely that his walk from Swanston to Glencorse Kirk and the " clinkum-clank o' Sabbath bells " attuned his imagination to find in the country folks and the surrounding countryside much of the material for " A Lowden Sabbath Morn." The eerie tree-bordered graveyard was an ideal place for such a tale as *The Body-Snatcher*, and the scene in *Weir of Hermiston* would seem to belong to the inside of the kirk—where Archie Weir first beheld Kirstie Elliot.

I am told by one who attended the church that Stevenson was fairly regular in attendance — about every second Sunday—and that on entering the gate the lanky lad with the velvet coat, whose appearance caused people to question each other as to who he was, would turn off the footpath to the right, and was frequently seen, just before the bell rang, examining the tombstones :

> " The prentit stanes that mark the deid,
>   Wi' lengthened lip, the sarious read ;
>   Syne wag a moraleesin' heid,
>   An' then an' there
>   Their hirplin' practice an' their creed
>   Try hard to square."

Then he would look over the wall to the burn that
" drums and pours in cunning whimples " in the glen
behind the kirk.

He noted

> " The solemn elders at the plate
> Stand drinkin' deep the pride o' State,"

as the congregation by ones and twos straggled slowly
in through the gateway and placed their " collection "
in the napkined plate.

There is no record that the " little house at the entering in of the church," referred to in the kirk-session
minutes, has any reference to the days of Burke and
Hare, although these nefarious scoundrels knew the
neighbourhood well. It was built in 1726, and was
used by the elders who stood there " to collect the
poor's money." It is described in the treasurer's
accounts as " the building of the porch in the church-
yard," and no doubt the steps at the side gate, now
worn to an interesting degree and lovingly noted by
every pilgrim, were built at the same time, so that for
over two hundred years the feet of pilgrims, worshipful
and otherwise, have passed in and out of the hallowed
place.

In the same year as " the little gatehouse " was built,
the session clerk, who was also schoolmaster and precentor, was appointed " to make a little tent for the
minister to preach in without at the time of the Sacrament." It was the custom in those days to come from
far and near to that solemn service, and as the kirk
could seldom accommodate all who came, a tent was
erected outside, in which the different ministers took turn
about in preaching, while the " tables " were being

served inside the kirk. And although this practice had ceased to exist in Stevenson's day he was doubtless aware of it, but he makes no reference to it. Had he been privileged to read the old session minutes, what a story of romance he might have woven around the old kirk—of the stories of the slaves in Algiers, for whose ransom collections were made ; of the great days of national fast, humiliation, and thanksgiving for British victories on the Continent ; and of the disturbed state of Glencorse parish at the end of the seventeenth century, when the fear of French invasion was widespread. The trials for sheep-stealing on the Pentlands would certainly have interested him, while the case of the defaulting parishioner who could not go to church " for want of cloaths," and justified his defiance of the holy men of session by saying " he was counselled to it," would not have failed his sense of humour.

But Stevenson says little that is of real interest about Glencorse, or about the minister of his day. One would have expected his versatile imagination to have laid hold upon the originality and the quaintness of Torrence's personality. He saw only the hole in the black gloves, and heard a voice that " leapt like an ill-played clarionet from key to key." Of the sermons he listened to, or of the old man's favourite text on charity, or of his prayers, he says nothing. Surely he must often have been arrested by the aptly chosen liturgy that the faithful steward adopted, suitably framed to meet the needs and the aspirations, the hopes and the fears, of his congregation, most of whom were interested in farming and agriculture. Nor would the anxiety of the shepherds' collie dogs to get out of the building as the benediction was being pronounced escape Stevenson's notice. I am assured that it was the case that frequently the words could not be heard because of the barking of the dogs, who seemed to know that the service was over—all but " the blessing."

On one occasion at least the solemnity of the congregation was greatly upset when a bird flew into the church, and after circling round for some time alighted upon the minister's head.   Mr. Torrence was unperturbed.   Slowly he raised his arm, keeping it close to his side, then he made a hasty " grab," but he was too late—the bird escaped, and all the congregation smiled.

And yet Stevenson's attendance at Glencorse made a real impression upon him, for did he not write to S. R. Crockett, then minister of Penicuik, " Oh, that I were the lad I once was sitting under old Torrence . . . I would even be willing to sit under you just to be there ! " " Just to be there "—yes, that's just it.   Some of life's experiences are felt too deeply ever to find utterance— sacred feelings that never find expression.   What Glencorse meant to Stevenson we shall never know.   But what he has given to us, and what he has left to the imagination, are sufficient to draw visitors to the old kirk from all over the world.

Chapter XIV

"GLENCORSE" LEGENDS

CURIOUS old legends gather round the names of the Pentland parish of Glencorse and the Pentland height of Carnethy. In the Statistical Account of the parish, written in 1845, the spelling " Glencross " was adopted, the reason given being that according to Chalmers in his *Caledonia*, the parish derived its name "from a remarkable cross which had once been erected in the Vale of Glencross by pious hands." It was admitted that the general modern spelling was Glencorse, but the writer appeared to believe that Glencross was the true and original name.

It is interesting, therefore, to endeavour to trace the various traditional legends which go to support the theory of the Glen of the Cross. The statement in Chalmers's *Caledonia* refers to a story that after the Battle of Roslin, in 1302, a cross was erected in the valley of Glencorse to mark the place where several of the English were buried, and that this cross gave name to the parish.

This bears some resemblance to Father Hay's story in the *Genealogie of the Saint Clairs of Roslin*, except that Father Hay makes it clear that none of the encounters between the Scots and English forces took place in this parish or in the immediate neighbourhood of Glencorse valley, while the cross mentioned by him was erected on the field of battle—" Att a place in the moore (Roslin Moor) named Bilsdone burne . . . they became victors, slew Rodolph their Generall ; the death of whom, after it came to the ears of a lady in England, who intirely loved him, she made be sett up in remembrance of his death in that part a crosse of stone. . . . The ground whereon the battle was fought, the first of them at Bilsdone burne, besides Draidone . . . the other two betwixt Draidone and Hethornden. . . ."

So the statement in Chalmers's *Caledonia* does not receive any historical support from Father Hay's *Genealogie*.

In the *Tales of Roslin Castle* (1836), by Jackson, we have a more elaborate story.

The English army arrives unexpectedly at Roslin, and information is at once sent by the prior of Mount Lothian to Sir Simon Fraser at Neidpath, who instructs Sir John Cummin and other leaders to assemble their forces at Biggar. In due course the Scots army of 8,000, with Sir Simon in command, ride out from Biggar on the way to Roslin. At Carlops they are joined by 500 Knights of St. John, a powerful body of military ecclesiastics, whose preceptory was at Torphichen, and who had come over the Pentlands to lend their aid to the Scots army. The troops are addressed at Carlops by the prior of the monastery at Newhall, Robert Abernethy.

The Battle of Roslin comprised victories over three sections of the English army of 30,000 men. After the march from Biggar, and the fighting of two battles, the troops were wellnigh exhausted, but the prior comes to their aid. He again addresses the Scots army, exhorting them to continue the fight, and pointing out what would happen if they were defeated—how they would be degraded and forced to be slaves—and calling upon them to fight for their king and country and all that they held dear, and affirming that if shortly they would cast their eyes towards the highest pinnacle of the Pentlands, then, as a sign of Heaven's assistance and victory in the fight, they would observe that an angel from on high had torn an oak from the hill and formed it into a cross, which, amidst the clouds of heaven, would brighten in the wind.

Ten thousand English horsemen appear rushing for the battlefield, and with one accord the Scots lift up their eyes to the hills, and then the cry, " A miracle ! A miracle ! The Cross, the Cross of Heaven is on the hill ! To arms ! To arms ! " So victory is secured.

The story then goes on to narrate how the hill on the Pentlands on which the miraculous cross appeared with such wonderful effect was, in honour of the prior, named Abernethy Hill, but from the large cairn of stones accumulating upon it—brought thither by the many devout pilgrims who visited the spot—its name was ultimately changed from Abernethy to Carnethy, which it still remains.

After the battle the cross was carried from the hill, down the valley, and deposited in a house for inspection by soldiers and visitors, the house thereafter being named Cross-house, now the name of the farm adjoining Glencorse Manse. Such is the romantic story of the Cross in the Glen.

Unfortunately this story, like that of Chalmers's *Caledonia*, does not account for the real name of the parish.

The legend bears some resemblance to that of the appearance of the Cross of St. Andrew. In that case Hungus, King of the Picts, with 30,000 warriors, assisted by 10,000 Scots under Prince Alpine, met the Saxons under Athelstan, bent on conquest, on the banks of a stream near the pastoral hills of Dirleton. Picts and Scots were hushed in prayer as they knelt to pray for victory over the Saxons. Despite the valour of both, the Saxons were prevailing, when lo ! a black thundercloud appeared on the eastern horizon, the lightning flashed, the thunder growled. Then the clouds opened, and above the Scottish host there appeared in a blaze of light the figure of St. Andrew, the apostle, on his cross, the two beams tied like the letter X. Inspired by this omen the Picts and Scots rushed to victory, and St. Andrew became the patron saint of Scotland. This legend dates from about the end of the eighth century.

As to the name of the Pentland height—Carnethy— an effort has been made to connect it with Car or Caer, a fortress, and Nectan or Nethan, a Pictish king, the Picts having possessed this neighbourhood at an early date, and upon this hill was situated Nethan's fortress. But what of the cairn of stones ? For this is no ordinary cairn, and could not have been erected after the Battle of Roslin as the story fancifully describes, because this cairn is a genuine " hilltop " cairn belonging to the Bronze Age. The name may signify Carneddau, the plural of Carnedd, a heap of stones.

Such cairns, as we have seen, have always been regarded as possessing some religious significance, as also do the stone circle at Marchwell and the cup-and-ring marked stone at Glencorse Church.

The whole parish, indeed, has been a centre of religious

worship from the earliest times. The Chapel of St. Katherine's is said to date from the thirteenth century; its site now covered by the waters of Glencorse. Hoolets' Hoose in the Logan Valley, considered to have been the abode of a priest—perhaps in connection with St. Katherine's—but latterly a ruin frequented by owls, is said to date from the sixteenth century, and no satisfactory date has yet been fixed when Glencorse Kirk first existed. And while all this may in part explain the desire to have the parish and the glen associated with a cross, it does not amount to any definite historical evidence.

Yet another origin for the name has been suggested. Watson in his *Celtic Place Names in Scotland* gives " Glencorse, Glencroskt, 1336 (Bain's *Calendar*), the Glen of the Crossings; there are three different old crossings, all of them rights-of-way "—and this appears plausible, and is indeed to some extent supported by facts. There are the right-of-way up the Glen to Bavelaw—reputed at one time to have been a hunting seat; the crossing between Scald Law and Carnethy known as the " Kirk Road "; and the old drove road from Currie across the Glen to the markets at House o' Muir and Turnhouse. The first was doubtless merely a cross-country road to Bavelaw and the Temple lands of Calder and Torphichen; the second was the road to Penicuik, used when St. Katherine's was joined to that parish in 1636; while the third was a drove road to the markets; but not one of the three is old enough to account for the name as the Glen of the Crossings.

Dr. Milne gives it as the Glen that Crosses the Pentland range, and Johnston, in his *Place Names in Scotland*, describes it as " The Glen of the Heath or Corse."

The truth is that the original name is not Glencross but Glencorse, written indifferently from time to time as " cors," " corss," " corsse," " corce," and " corse," but never " cross." Glencorse has been the name of the parish and barony and estate from the thirteenth century, and has been uniformly adopted in Acts of Parliament, royal charters, title deeds, public registers, and other authentic books and documents. The question arose acutely when the new railway station came to be named and when the name of Greenlaw Barracks was changed, and at that time Lord Justice General Inglis (afterwards Lord President) wrote a pamphlet (December 26, 1877) giving evidence which he had collected proving the name to be Glencorse and not Glencross, from which it appears that in the year 1259, forty-three years before the Battle of Roslin, Hugh, the son of Sir Patrick Abernethy, gave, with his sister in marriage, to Hugh de Douglas, twenty merk lands in the " town of Glencorse in Edinburgh."

The name Glencorse is a well-known though not very common Scottish surname, and like many another Scottish surname was in all probability derived from the name of a place.

Chapter XV

A ROYAL DEER HUNT

IN the ancient manuscript *The Genealogie of the Saint Clairs of Roslin* there is a record of a royal hunt upon the Pentland Hills in which King Robert the Bruce staked the estate of Pentland and the forest of Pentland Moor against the life of Sir William Saint Clair, on the result of the hunt of a white faunch deer by Sir William and his two hounds " Help " and " Hold."

Since this genealogy was compiled by Father Hay, who finished his collections in 1700, many chroniclers have retold the story of the royal hunt, and in the course of time the tradition has been woven into a story of picturesque description and romantic association, with all the sparkling glitter of old-world chivalry.

In the days of King Robert hunting was attended with much splendour, and after the Battle of Bannockburn, when the public mind was once more freed from the anxiety attendant upon defensive warfare, the sport of the chase was again taken up, and prosecuted with the same vigour as the Scots had thrown into the art of war. The surroundings of Edinburgh were particularly well adapted for this, and the favourite fields and forest extended west from the Borough-muir and across the Pentlands into Linlithgow and Lanarkshire, and east from the Pentlands to the Moorfoots and into Tweed-dale.

After Bannockburn King Robert found recreation and enjoyment in hawking and the chase, hunting with his nobles in that part of the country which extends from Mount Lothian and Roslin along the south of the Pentland range. The royal stables and kennels were at the south back of the Castle, in the West Port, where the name " King's Stables Road " still remains. The meeting-place of hounds and huntsmen was the Buck Stane, a large block of granite which may still be seen, built into the wall nearly opposite Mortonhall Golf Clubhouse in Old Braid Road, and from there the favourite route was by the village of Pentland, a noted hunting centre, to the hunting ground of Mount Lothian.

The story goes that arrangements had been made for a special day in the hunting fields, the king being desirous of testing the speed of his best pack of hounds and the mettle of his finest hunters. Accordingly, one summer morning, the king and a large retinue of his nobility from all the strongholds in the Lothians, with hounds and huntsmen, assembled at the Buck Stane. Here the huntsman wound the bugle horn, and the royal party moved forward in the direction of Mount Lothian, where on previous occasions a stag had been found to provide the chase in the king's forest.

On this bright day the king and all his lords and ladies, a merry and a valiant throng, were keen and excited for the chase. The hounds are laid on to the sound of the horn, and the forest rings with the joyful note. A shout goes up from a hundred voices as the stag bounds from cover. The hounds are uncoupled, and the whole field is in pursuit.

Bounding over the undulating countryside, the stag takes over the Esk, mounts the rising ground to " House of Muir," crosses the Linton road, breaks off to the right at Turnhouse—the house where the stag turned—continues over the gently sloping ground to the Logan Glen, and heads for the narrowing outlet, now covered by Glencorse Reservoir. The hunters are close behind the stag, the hounds are at the point of snatching at its haunches, when, with a bound, it clears the March Burn, darts in among the scattered brushwood, gaining ground from its pursuers, and escapes through a pass on the north side of the hills.

If the stag can gain the pass and reach the forest its life is safe ; and so there ensues a fierce struggle. Sir William Saint Clair and Randolph de Clerc and other noble huntsmen are close in pursuit, the king and several members of the royal suite have lost ground, and are some way behind. Will the stag reach the forest ? Here in this open field, through the cleuch in the hills, is witnessed all the poetry of motion of the chase ; time and again the stag eludes its pursuers until, with the swiftness of the wind, one desperate effort is made, and it gains the cover of the forest. The hunt is over, and the hounds are recalled, after a run of nearly ten miles.

It is out of the circumstances attending this chase that the famous wager arises. As the king approaches it is noted that he appears to be displeased. He who had once been hunted as a stag knew what it was to win through to victory, but this defeat was unpleasant to him. He was the spectator of a hunt in which not only he himself had been defeated, but his famous hounds had been outstripped by a deer, and that in as

GLENCORSE KIRK IN STEVENSON'S DAY.

GLENCORSE RESERVOIR.

fair a chase as could have been desired. Moreover, was
not this the same white faunch deer that had beat the
hounds on a previous occasion ? Could it be that the
steed of Saint Clair was faster than his own, since he
had finished far behind the knight, and were the hounds
of Saint Clair fleeter than those of the king ?

The assembled nobility, observing his mood, endeavour to turn aside the matter, and laugh good-
naturedly as if to hearten His Majesty, whereat the
knight momentarily flushes, then answers sharply that
if a test is wished of the speed and mettle of Sir William's
hounds, he would stake his head if the hounds failed to
kill the same stag before it crossed the March Burn at
the foot of Clachmede, wind and weather being favourable, and such other regulations to do him justice as
the appointed judges might think proper.

To this His Majesty agrees, but adds that he values
the life of Saint Clair more highly than the noble knight
apparently does himself, so he stakes the forest of Pentland Moor, the best at his disposal, against Sir William's
head, but bids him recollect that, should he lose, his life
must pay the penalty of his rashness. And this was no
rash wager, let it be remembered, but an act of chivalry
in which our Scottish knights and yeoman of old loved
to engage from time to time, and in which they strove
to excel, for some fair reward. Whereupon it is agreed
that one week hence the noblemen will assemble at the
Buck Stane at eight in the morning, and ride to take
their station with the king on the Pentland Hills to
view the vital chase. The place where this wager was
made was a farm called " Threap Moor "—" to threap,"
being to maintain by dint of assertion, to maintain
persistently, to argue.

Soon the day arrived. From an early hour a great concourse of people made their way from Edinburgh and the surrounding districts to the Pentlands, and, marshalled by the royal officers, took up their positions according to their rank on the slopes and summits of the hills. At ten o'clock on this summer morning the king and his retinue were at their stations on the King's Hill, near Kirkton, and with him were the Bishop of Dunkeld, the Earl of Orkney and Stratherne, and Lady Elizabeth de Spar (the anxious lover of the chivalrous knight), Lady Catherine Saint Clair, and other ladies from the castles of Dirleton, Dalhousie, and Roslin. Nearer the fateful burn stood the judges.

Meantime at the starting-point excitement is growing. Cleland, the head huntsman of Roslin, with the slow-hounds is moving to get behind the stag, so that the desired route might be taken. Then follows his bugle blast and the baying of the hounds, the stag is started, and quickly bounding from the covert of the forest passes near where the knight and his party stand ready, the knight having previously implored the divine protection and that of the Blessed Virgin and Saint Katherine. The hounds are slipped, Sir William mounts his steed, accompanied by his friend Randolph de Clerc, and all are off on the momentous chase. The Esk is crossed half a mile west of Auchendinny, where a kill almost takes place, which would have spoiled the glorious holiday of the waiting thousands at Glencorse, but at Beeslack the stag gains ground and mounts the heights till " House of Muir " is reached, and the course then followed is similar to that of the previous hunt. It is a hard chase. Along the edge of the burn the stag runs, the noble huntsmen following hard upon hounds and cheering them on. Through the bottle-neck they race to the open arena in full view of the king and the assembled multitude. During these tense moments the spectators stand spellbound, and there is a silence as of death.

They are now within two hundred yards of the March Burn and the Copsewood. The hounds renew their effort, and at thirty yards, so close are they upon the stag, the excited multitude, king, judges, and all, think that they have hold upon it, but the stag keeps on, and as it dashes into the burn a horrified groan surges from a thousand throats. Is the life of the brave knight forfeit, and " hath a rose fallen from his chaplet "? Events take place quickly. It seems the knight thought that all was over, and sprang from his horse to surrender his life, but he had judged too quickly, for, like a lightning flash de Clerc charges past him, and at the same moment as the stag enters the burn " Hold " fastens his teeth in its hind leg. It stumbles, " Help " rushes in front of the stag and turns it upon the knight's side, when the two hounds kill it upon the haugh, and save their master's life.

Loud and long were the shouts of joy that reverberated along the peaks of the Pentland glen. As the judges come forward to congratulate Sir William and de Clerc, the king descends from the hill, Lady Elizabeth de Spar, the betrothed of Sir William on his right, and Lady Catherine Saint Clair, betrothed of Randolph de Clerc, on his left. A circle is formed upon the haugh, afterwards called the " Knights Field," the two huntsmen in the centre, and the king receives the verdict that all has been done to the judges' satisfaction. Whereupon His Majesty places the hand of Lady de Spar into that of Sir William, saying, " Sir William, your wager is most honourably won ; you have saved your life and I give you in perpetuity and free forestrie the estate of Pentland and Pentland Moor, with the whole of the Pentland range of hills, bounded by Hillend on the east, and the Esk at Carlops on the west, as lasting memorials of this glorious hunt, and may the Almighty grant you and the lovely Elizabeth long life and happiness to enjoy these estates."

Turning then to Randolph de Clerc, the king joins the hand of Lady Saint Clair to that of her lover, and narrates the noble services and sacrificing vicissitudes of his family in Scotland's cause, and desiring that reparation and reward should be made to him he grants the estate of Pennecuik to march with the Pentland range belonging to Sir William Saint Clair, to be held on the tenure " that when I or any of the succeeding kings of Scotland shall come to hunt upon the Pentlands or Borough-muir your forester shall attend at the gathering, and, sitting upon the top of the Buck Stane, near Edinburgh, shall wind three blasts of the bugle horn." Then, drawing his sword and touching the shoulder of de Clerc, he dubs him knight and says, " Arise, Sir Randolph de Clerc of Pennecuik." The news quickly spreads among the serried ranks of spectators on the hillsides, and once more the hills resound to cheers, renewed again and again.

That this day of the royal hunt of Midlothian and the Pentland Hills was a day long to be remembered is shown by the local tradition which has carried the story down through the centuries to the present day, for the story of " Help " and " Hold " is still told in this Midlothian countryside in castle and in cottage, where dogs for

ST. KATHERINE'S IN THE HOPES : SUBMERGED CHAPEL RUINS.

(Photographed 22nd October 1933.)

hunting and for sheep have upheld for generations a reputation that is world-wide.

The family history of the Saint Clairs, the memoirs of the Clerks, the poetical writings of Sir Walter, and the historical romance in Jackson's *Chivalry of Scotland and the Royal Hunt of Roslin*, which have been followed in the foregoing narrative, bear witness to the story based on local tradition. That the lands in the Moor of Pentlande were conveyed to the Saint Clairs is established by the following charter, entered in the Register of the Great Seal, and dated April 12, 1316:

"Charter by King Robert I. granting to Henry of St. Clair, Knight, for his homage and service, all our land in the Moor of Pentlande with pertinents; to be held by him and his heirs from the Crown in fee and heritage with all pertinents by which the said lands were accustomed to be held in the time of the King's predecessor (Alexander III.); granting, moreover, that the said Henry and his heirs shall have, hold, and possess the said land for ever in free warren, discharging hereby all persons to cut wood, use hawking or hunting in the said lands, without licence from the said Henry and his heirs, under pain of forfeiture; rendering therefor the tenth part of a knight's service in battle, and three suits yearly at the Sheriff's Court held at Edinburgh."

The traditional story is one that all lovers of the Pentland Hills, of historical romance, and of true chivalry would gladly believe to be true.

Chapter XVI

"QUEEN OF THE RESERVOIRS"

THE amphitheatre in the hills in which the closing scene of the preceding romantic story of the royal deer hunt took place now contains a picturesquely environed lake into which flow the Logan Burn and other hillside rills and streams. On several occasions, however, it has become dried up in droughts, and excellent facilities then became available for the study of its construction and geological formation.

Special difficulties were met with in making the dam which intercepts the surplus water of the valley streams, owing to the necessity of reaching the solid rock. The bed of gravel that had to be removed was 53 feet in depth, and in removing it the ground on the south side, consisting of loose and somewhat friable felspathic trap, fell in and retarded the work. The embankment across the glen is 128 yards in length, 140 yards in thickness at the base, and slopes gradually to the top, 130 feet above the former level of the stream. Through the embankment two great tunnels were built, one at the lower end giving out the water required for mills on the Esk to compensate for the loss of the Crawley Water ; the other, the " safety " tunnel near the top, to let off flood water, and these form at times two beautiful cascades as the water falls into its former channel. The work, which occupied 300 men for three years, and cost £209,000, was completed in 1822, and was considered one of the most important gravitation water works of the time. The waters of Glencorse and Crawley Spring are mixed in a cistern near Flotterstane Brig, and the combined supply is filtered at Alnwickhill, and conveyed by the Crawley pipe laid in 1819 to the terminus at Queen Street, Edinburgh. Between the Meadows and the Grassmarket, and between the Grassmarket and the Mound, the pipe is laid in tunnels driven through solid rock. A branch pipe connects with the reservoir on the Castlehill. Glencorse is now connected with the Talla Aqueduct, and acts as a service reservoir in connection with the Talla scheme. Owing to severe drought in the summer of 1933 the reservoir was again almost dry, and the unusual spectacle attracted many visitors.

The most interesting treatise on Glencorse is that contained in an article by Hugh Miller on the Droughts of 1842. He resided for some time at Roslin, knew the Pentlands well, and described the reservoir as marked by all the characteristics of a genuine Highland loch in a genuine Highland glen, surrounded by bold steep banks embosomed among hills varying from 1,000 to 1,900 feet in height.

" It was not every day," he wrote, " that one could walk dry shod over the bottom of a lake a full mile in length, and not less than ten fathoms deep. All above the bank is brown with heath and withered fern, all beneath is browner still with sludge, gravel, and mud; but a rectilinear bar of lighter colour runs along the high water line where the light of day and the water of the lake have been operating during the last twenty years in bleaching the various earths and stones on which for that period they have been beating together. In the midst there rises a pyramid of hardened mud, piled over the tombstone of James Glendinning (1666) to protect it from the ravages of the class who entertain so thorough a regard for interesting monuments of antiquity that they always carry them away piecemeal in their pockets unless prevented by force. On the ridge of the eminence we see a low brown parallelogram, as if cast in clay, some forty feet by twenty or so. And these form the entire remains of the Chapel of St. Katherine's in the Hopes and its burying ground." On each occasion when the reservoir becomes dry, the evidences of the Chapel and tombstones suffer by depredation until very few now remain.

Referring to the practically dry reservoir, Miller goes on to say that all marks of life have not ceased. " In even the lowest depths the surface is studded over with minute, dark-coloured specks like pinheads, and it is perceived on examination that these minute specks are shell-fish. The surface is covered by millions and thousands of millions of that delicate bivalve, the cyclas. All are dead ; the mollusc within exists but as a minute, blackish speck of decaying animal matter. Mark, further, that though the shell of a univalve—a lymnea or valvata—is occasionally met with, these are comparatively rare, and not in the proportion of one for every one thousand of the other class. We must not too hastily infer, however, that the bivalves were by much the more abundant inhabitants of the lake. They were only worse fitted by nature for retreat than their neighbours. They were fixed by nature to the place which they now occupy, and when left by the receding waters they died ; whereas the univalves marched

downwards as the waters fell, and may now be found
by myriads in the patch of a few acres into which the
lake has contracted its limits. What a puzzle for
future geologists ! In this layer of shells they will find
scarce anything but bivalves. In the layer that will
be deposited above it, it is probable that univalves will
be the more numerous. Or suppose that the whole
lake were to dry up, and that with all the bivalves all
the univalves were to perish also. How account for
the vast accumulation of the latter in one spot, as
opposed to the equal diffusion of the other class ? How
very difficult a riddle, and yet how easily read with the
assistance of the key."

As Miller saw it in 1842, the terraced beaches of the
lake—parallel roads—were in some places remarkably
well defined. " We walked for several hundred yards
along one of the beaches, dug by waves out of a steep
slope of about thirty-five degrees, where the terrace
was fully six feet in breadth, and declined at so low an
angle that it made no unpleasant road. At another
place we counted no fewer than eighteen of these terraces varying from a few feet to a few inches in breadth,
in a declivity of not more than fifty feet. Like those
pencillings of the ventometer through which the winds
are made to register their own power and direction,
they served to indicate what gales had prevailed during
the various stages when the waters were sinking, and
with what force they had blown."

The general appearance of the bottom of the pond,
with its footprints of men and animals still uneffaced,
is described in his *Sketchbook of Popular Geology*, Lecture
V., which should be perused by all Pentland Walkers
geologically inclined.

Chapter XVII

"THE OLD ROAD"—A REVERIE

THE old roads round the hills, whether they be no longer highways but grass-grown and used only by the country folks, the village merchant, and the wayfaring man who loves the road that has gone back to Nature, or have become modern highways that supersede the centuries-old turnpike, are equally interesting to the sensitive and contemplative mind. The way of each may be stamped with personality.

Let us sit upon the heathery hillside and enjoy our reverie of one of these old roads that lies hidden in the shelter of the hills.

We have before us an old grass-grown road ; on one side there is a grassy bank and a wood of tall pines, the other side is open to the hills—a wide view in which, at evening, the far heights take on a deep dark blue that is almost black. In the foreground is the green grass and the brown earth around the red-roofed farm steading, while in the middle distance, under a grove of wind-swept pines, there is a stream that tells its story as long as you will listen. Facing west the hills form a wide semicircle. In this vast area the scenery—the atmosphere—changes momentarily in the still, quiet spring evenings. And while this is happen-

ing there is an orchestra in the woods. The Spirit of
the Hills haunts the place—it broods over the valley—
it sings in the trees—it lives in the Old Road itself. And
it speaks to us quietly at times, and here is what it
says :

"Where are the wheels of the old mail coach I knew
so well, that rattled along—up along, down along, out
along—to the old inn near by ? Where is the horn that
broke the stillness of the hills ? Where is all the bustle
at the old inn door—the jingling of steel bits, of traces
and harness, the noise of pails and ostlers' hobnailed
boots on cobblestones ? Where is the sound of the
cheery greetings of mine hosts—Old Douglas, Old
Purdie, Old Graham—and where is Old Wedderspuine
who hobnobbed with royalty and with royal plotters ?
And where are my Lords Traquair, Linton, and Tweeddale, who stayed in the inn on the Lord's Day instead
of paying their vows in the Parish Kirk, and had to
answer for it to the session ?

"Kings and queens many have I known. Did not the
gay and light-hearted James stop here to dine ere he went
to Cramalt to the hunting ; and the last of the Bourbons
—he toasted his toes in the inn at the end of the day's
sport at Slipperfield ? Did not Mary, the Queen of
Scots, newly betrothed, ride past upon a gallant steed,
with Darnley by her side—and a gay equipage with
pennons streaming in the October sunshine—on to
Biggar, to be welcomed by eighteen thousand loyal
hearts, nobles, barons, knights, and retainers, from every
part of the kingdom ? And the ' Lords of the Congregation '—here they sealed their plot before they set
off for Stirling by the ancient drove road through the
Cauldstaneslap to obtain satisfaction from the king.

And in procession upon the Old Road I see that warrior, Edward I.—'Longshanks' we called him—riding with his army from the Hills of Braid bound for Linton Roderick and the West Country; and farther back still I see the Scottish army riding to Roslin to defeat the English in the Scottish Wars of Independence."

And hardly a name in the brave list of those we love in Scottish literature but knew the Old Road well —Allan Ramsay, Robert Burns, Sir Walter, "Rab and his Friends," R. L. S., and all the rest.

The Old Road was busy in the August days of '22, for they were days of rejoicing, when another king, the fourth of the Georges, landed from the Firth to greet the subjects of his new-found kingdom—there they went, old and young, rich and poor, eager to reach the capital to catch a glimpse of His Majesty—farmers in blue coats and broad-brimmed hats, knee-breeches and brass-buckled shoes, riding upon hairy ponies; hill shepherds with blue bonnets, tartan plaids, and faithful collie dogs, and ploughmen with ribboned gaiters and clay-covered shoes.

And not only did the royal mail bound along with its four fine horses and its red-coated guard sounding his horn—past Fairslacks, Waterloo, and Trafalgar, where cottagers were gathered, but there were also slower vehicles—carriers' carts in which sat dear old women in white mutches, black snoods, and velvet brow-bands, and buxom, ruddy-faced lassies with Sunday mutches edged wi' lace, tippets o' white, and frocks o' red and green. And in keeping with its dignity and romance the yellow painted stage coach kept an even pace as it passed group after group upon the dusty road, affording to the eager travellers a momentary glimpse

SLIPPERFIELD.

" RESPITE AND NEPENTHE."

of powder-wigged flunkies outside, and the great lord and his gentle lady inside—and only a hundred years ago !

Where are they all now ? All gone ! All gone ! but all alive ; and the Old Road, too, is still alive, folded in the bosom of Mother Nature, to whom it began to go back in '33, when they made the new road and built the new inn. All the personality of the travellers of all the ages has been woven into the Old Road. What scenes have been enacted upon it, what deeds of valour and courage, ignominy and shame, high-hearted love and frowning hate, light tripping footsteps and heavy, weary feet, gaiety of marriage and sorrow of mourning, dawns and sunsets of red and gold, bright noons and starry nights, and the whole round of life and death through the revolving seasons of the years.

Like old persons richly wise in life's experience, the Old Road has absorbed all the story and the mystery of human life. If only the road would tell us its tale, difficult and complex though it might be for our understanding ! Ah ! but its revelation comes to us in strange manner ; we are enlightened just a little at a time. The Spirit of the Old Road, like the Spirit of the Hills, is always there ; it haunts the place and broods over it, although the road itself may seem to remain silent, sphinx-like. The favoured ones will always meet some one there on this old highway, though no person is visible ; it is the Spirit of the Old Road—very friendly, a friend who will go with you all the way. That is why we are drawn by some strange invisible magnet to visit the Old Road, to saunter slowly along its wild, reedy, grass-grown borders, and lean over the old wayside gates that lead out to the whinny braes, just on the chance that we may catch something of the Spirit of the travelling road to carry back with us.

It is sweet to linger there in the freshness of the dawn, when the road radiates a softness and a kindliness that attracts the " jumping things " from the wayside coverts, and when the morning light strikes the road the very soul of sound seems to be abroad, so vibrant is the light, and there is movement too in the undulations of the road.

In the hours of sunset and of gloaming and the fading of daylight into dark—those mystic hours whose secret is shared with the twinkling stars—there are strange movements on the Old Road, a restlessness ere the quiet of night settles down upon it. There are moving shadows, fingers of gaunt trees and plumes of pines, the rhythmic nodding of horses' heads, and above the formless figures of horsemen and of warriors riding onwards, the flittermouse is flying and the owlets are calling.

Surely, we will say, in the still, clear, frosty moonlight, when even Nature's breath is hushed, the Old Road must be asleep. Yes, it may be asleep, but dreaming of other days—the clamp and ring of horses' feet, the rolling and rumbling of wheels and the startling horn, the creaking of country carts, the lowing of cattle, the voices of men—and there is a tramping and a marching too ! And as the moonlight pales before the first faint streaks of dawn, elfin figures retiring from their revels upon the Old Road pass to the grove above the river's bank. True, there is nothing visible, no sound is heard in the white ghostly silence, so softly did it fall upon the inner ear. It was the Spirit of the Old Road, retelling his story.

For, after all, it is a spirit world in which we live ; and it is by some such favoured Old Road that we reach the Temple of the Hills in which our hearts uprise.   It may even be that, led by the Spirit of the Old Road, we find the way to our Arcadia—that land of delight where human needs are met and satisfied by the great simple things of life—the love and friendship of all who breast with us the upward road.

Chapter XVIII

SOME WHIMSICAL LAIRDS

THE road between Leadburn and Romanno is now a modern highway, but it still retains its romantic atmosphere because of the countryside through which it passes. It is the old coach road from Edinburgh to Moffat and Dumfries by Auchendinny, Howgate, Romanno, and the Crook Inn—a main turnpike to the South from early times. It overlooks the Harlaw Moor, and commands a far-spreading view of the Pentland range.

The inns at Leadburn and Noblehouse were well known to travellers, and both were in existence in the seventeenth century. Leadburn Inn is mentioned in John Buchan's romance of that period, *John Burnet of Barns*, in which it is described as a villainous bleak place, standing in the middle of a black peat bog in a forsaken countryside, but the landlord was an active, civil man, and the laird obtained an excellent dinner— a brace of wild fowl and a piece of salted beef " washed down with a very tolerable wine." It was here that he was joined by Nicol Plenderleith, the loyal and devoted servant who accompanied him in all his travels. On his return from Holland he is advised by a footpad at Leadburn to " haud doon by the Brochton and New-

ENTRANCE STEPS, GLENCORSE KIRK.

GOLDIE'S MILL.

lands ways, for a' the way atween Leidburn and Peebles is hotchin wi' sodgers."

In William Black's *Strange Adventures of a Phæton,* written in the latter half of the nineteenth century, the inn is referred to as a cut-throat-looking place, a dingy, dilapidated building standing at a parting of two roads. " It looked like one of those remote and gloomy inns in the annals of romance." Nevertheless the travellers obtained both food and stimulant that enabled them to complete in comfort the last stage of the journey from London to Edinburgh.

The inn stands at an elevation of 900 feet above sea-level, and at the time of Mr. Buchan's story the country was still " a virginal wilderness of heather and bog," but by draining and cultivation and the planting of trees the nature of the surrounding countryside has been changed during the last century, and although there are times when the encircling hills and moorlands wear a bleak and awesome aspect, there are other times when the woods and heathery valleys, the bracing hill air, the glorious clear-cut ridge of Pentland, and the blue hills of Tweeddale are as satisfying as the homely fare at the inn.

In the mail-coach days the inn at Noblehouse was the last stage in the journey from the South before reaching Edinburgh, and here horses were changed. The County Records of 1636 make reference to it. Some time after 1768 a Linton innkeeper, George Dalziel, took over Noblehouse, and Findlater, the clerical historian, says that Dalziel was the first farmer to sow turnips in the open fields and cultivate potatoes on a large scale. One of the landlords, the whimsical George Williamson, bequeathed the use of his hearse to the parishoners of Newlands in 1848.

(3,839)

9

The road would also be known to Tobias Smollett, who visited his mother at Scotstoun, west of Romanno, in 1755, after he had completed his *Don Quixote*, and after an absence of sixteen years. The family wished to surprise the old lady, whose son had been absent from her so long, and it was arranged that he should be introduced as a serious-looking gentleman from the West Indies, who was well known to her son ; but the game did not succeed. The mother's affection was not to be deceived, Tobias smiled, and the old lady sprang from her chair, and throwing her arms around him exclaimed, " Ah, my son ! my son ! I have found you at last ! " and afterwards added that if he had maintained an austere look she might perhaps have been deceived a little longer, but " your old roguish smile betrayed you at once ! "

The roads of the sixteenth and seventeenth centuries were far from being safe for travellers, and even in the heyday of the stage-coach in the eighteenth century danger of assault and robbery lurked on every side. It is recorded that the lands bordering this road were in the sixteenth century not safe to live upon " owing to the incursions of Border thieves," and the Romanno lands were " barren and subject to the incursionis and stouthis by the broken men and thieves of baith the Bordouris." In monastic times the lands called the Kingside Edge, beyond Noblehouse, belonged to the monks of Newbattle, and in 1532 the lands of Deanhouses, which supported the deans of the abbey, could neither grow grain nor support cattle for the same reason.

A hundred years later (1627) Deanhouses sends two representatives to the Weapon-schaw on the King's Muir at Peebles, " horsit, with jack, steil bonnet, sword and lance." A hundred and fifty years later (1782) a tenant of Deanhouses is the first in Tweeddale to begin dairy farming, and to send his produce to Edinburgh, thus showing that on the farms as well as on the roads there was a growing sense of security through the centuries to both life and property.

Rush and hurry were then unknown. Commerce had dignity and ease, and the droning of the water-wheel became one with the winds from the moor and the song of the birds in the trees. Goldie's Mill, near Romanno, existed before 1750, but is now dismantled, although there remain the wheel, the worn flags and steps, the loft where the grain was stored, and the stream where the horse drank and lifted his head with joy. It is clothed with a garment of beauty, rich tones radiate from its walls, birds regard it as a friendly place, tall grasses wave around it, and reflections in the stream change with the fleeting clouds. The old mill is silent ; but beauty never dies.

In the journey from Leadburn to Romanno the first mansion on the west is The Whim. Originally the site contained the herd's house of Blairbog, wet, marshy, boggy land surrounding it on all sides. The Earl of Islay discovered the place—it afforded excellent sport in wild duck and moor game—so he set about the task of turning a deep flaw-moss into a pleasant country seat. His courage was equalled by his sense of humour. Neighbours and friends laughed at the idea, and the earl enjoyed the laugh also, but worked at the same time. The more he worked, the more he smiled ; the bogland was becoming a garden, the whimsical idea was becoming fact. He drained the land, formed a lake, planted beech, laurel, spruce, and silver firs, erected a mansion house, and humorously called the place The Whim—and so it has remained from the day when it first so appeared in the Crown Charter of 1743. For some years the Earl (afterwards 3rd Duke) of Argyll used it as a convenient half-way house between Inveraray and London. He disposed of it in 1750 to his cousin, Lieut.-General Campbell of Mamore, the 4th Duke, who in turn sold it in 1763 to James Montgomery, advocate, younger son of Sir William Montgomery of Macbiehill, for, it is said, a very small sum ; in fact the estate cost him very little, so the story runs, when he came to reckon the value of the wine which was found in the cellars. But Dr. Chambers likened the house to a city hospital that had got strangely out of place, and considered that the court of stables and offices were " of an architectural exterior worthy of the palace of a German principality."

The next house to The Whim on the old coach road is Lamancha—a name given by an early proprietor belonging to the Dundonald family, who had lived for some time in the province of La Mancha in Spain. The whimsicality at once translates us to the realm of Don Quixote—and this district was not always destitute of windmills and knights in armour, for a certain proprietor in 1802, Captain Cochrane of H.M.S. *Ajax*, dug iron ore out of the neighbouring hills, carted it to a factory erected by him in the grounds, and by means of a calcining furnace and a water-driven wheel tried to make a dark red paint out of the ochres—whether for the painting of warships or windmills is not divulged. The experiment, however, proved a failure, and was discontinued. Another proprietor, James Mackintosh, a Banffshire Anglo-Indian, who acquired it in 1832, sunk coal pits, built lime kilns, and brick and tile works, provided a school, and was instrumental in securing the present railway station, which, alas! has recently been closed.

Prior to 1756 the estate was known as Romanno Grange, and was owned by the monks of Newbattle, who obtained possession of it in 1203 and retained it until the Reformation. This, undoubtedly, was a much better name than Lamancha, but they who had the choice knew better, for it was lacking surely in every sense of whimsicality—in other words it was not whimsical enough for the whimsical lairds whose lands marched with The Whim.

The adjoining estate of Macbiehill, formerly Coldcoat, also had a whimsical laird, Alexander Hamilton, macer to the Lords of Session. His cousin Jonas held the estate before him, and Jonas was a local celebrity, a soldier of Charles II., and a boon companion of Dr. Pennecuik, who wrote an Elegy upon him, and was no less genial and jovial than the other lairds of the district, but these friend-winning and companionable qualities were in some degree responsible for his disposal of the estate. In due course it came to Alexander, the macer, and he determined that in reconstructing the fortalice he would provide no fewer than fifteen sleeping-places, one for each of the fifteen judges who daily followed behind his mace in the Court of Session, so that all might be in session at Macbiehill at one and the same time. The room appointed for the President, who was nearest to him in every procession as well as in his affections, was double the size of the others, thus estimating, as was ingeniously suggested by the lawyer laird of Newhall, that one President was equal to two ordinary judges. But, alas! Alexander, the macer, forgot all about himself! No sleeping-place had been provided for him in the great house. Ah! but he had other plans —he intended to set his couch in the hall, so that he might keep watch over the sleeping judges through the night, and none be able to escape without his knowledge. And although they were never known to have done Alexander, the macer, any harm, it was whispered that not a few of them were indebted to him in large sums of money. Perhaps that is why eventually he had to part with the house and lands he loved so well.

Halmyre, once named Murrayshall, comes next. The powerful Baron Tweedie of Drummelzier built the house, and there seems to have been a feud between Tweedie's successor Murray, who obtained the lands in liquidation of a debt, and members of the Tweedie clan, for the latter attacked him with swords and other weapons and nearly killed him (1621). Ten years later one of the Murrays was cited by the Privy Council for murderous assault in Linton on one of the servants of the then laird, Wilkin Johnston. And if there be little that can be termed whimsical in the many merchant-burgess lairds of Halmyre, there is at least something pathetic in the saving clause that Alexander Murray inserted in the disposition in favour of his brother Walter, namely, that he should have the use of "a mid-chamber in the second storey and ane chamber in the third storey, also a stable and ane chamber above it" when he felt inclined to visit his former country house.

In 1803, however, Halmyre was owned by Mrs. Anne Murray Keith, who was no other than Mrs. Bethune Baliol of Sir Walter Scott's *Chronicles of the Canongate*—

that gentle, cultured lady of ancient and honourable family, to whom he was indebted, as he says, for the substratum of his Scottish fictions. To him her store of Scottish tradition was invaluable ; she could describe how Fletcher of Saltoun spoke, how Graham of Claverhouse danced, what jewels were worn by the famous Duchess of Lauderdale, and how she came by them. She could even remember the Highland clans being in Edinburgh, and satisfied Sir Walter that the chiefs " did not swagger about in plaids and broadswords at the Cross, or attend the Assembly Rooms in bonnets and kilts."

Some one suggested to Mrs. Baliol that as she was unable to occupy all the rooms in " Baliol's Lodging " in the Canongate, her town house, she should have the windows of the unused apartments built up to save the window tax, but with much ire she replied that while she lived the light of God should visit the house of her fathers, and while she had a penny king and country should have their due. And surely whimsicality could go no further than when she ordered that the income-tax collector should on calling be supplied with a glass of wine. The poor fellow was so overcome by the reception so unwontedly generous, that he wellnigh fainted on the spot !

Chapter XIX

CARLOPS TALES

The Weaver

A STORY was current among the old Carlops weavers of the occasion when one of their number graduated from apprentice to full-fledged journeyman, and of his experiences in endeavouring to secure a second-hand loom in the Canongate of Edinburgh, wherewith to set up in business in the Carlops.

It was customary for the young man to treat his fellow-'prentices to a supper, and on this occasion they held a feast of sheep's-head and haggis and potions of ale in the elder's house—the elder himself bespeaking a plaid as the weaver's first job after starting for himself. There was great fun and merriment, songs were sung, "Tam o' Shanter" and other poems recited, and many toasts given for the success, prosperity, and happiness of the host of the evening.

The young weaver had heard of great bargains in second-hand looms to be had at a certain shop in Edinburgh, and next day he started off to make his purchase. He came to the shop in high spirits, and was met by the proprietor, a lean-faced old fellow in knee-breeches, with a great gold chain and seals and keys hanging from his fob—an ill-favoured man, and if the weaver had not been so intent on his purpose he would have slipped away out of the shop without doing any business. The dealer was civil in his manner, however, when he asked him what he wanted, and on making his request known, was told he was just in the nick of time, because here was the very thing he required, almost new, that was to be sold that very day for £3, 10s.

The weaver was delighted at his good fortune, and looked over the loom carefully. Having been previously advised to bargain with the dealer and not to give the price first asked, he offered the shopman thirty shillings for it.

" I'll give it to you for three pounds," he replied ; " and not a penny less will I take," he added.

" No," said the weaver, " make it five-and-thirty shillings and I'll take it."

Then the price came down to forty-five shillings, but no further would the dealer go. The weaver was "sweered" to lose the chance ; he halved the difference, and the dealer agreed—" seeing he seemed a decent chiel, and he would like to encourage him."

So forty shillings was paid for the loom, and without delay it was put upon the carrier's cart for the Carlops. The carrier, too, said it was a capital bargain, although he thought it did look somewhat worm-eaten. The weaver walked by the side of the cart, with head erect, and proud of being the possessor of a loom, and of having made such a good bargain. How all the other 'prentices in the Carlops would envy him now !

When they got to Fairmilehead the carrier suggested that the weaver might get up on the cart and have a seat inside the four posts of the loom. Soon the happy weaver was sound asleep. Some time afterwards he

awoke with a start, and a certain gruesome feeling!
What was that? One look upon his sleeve was enough!
The weaver sprang up with such vigour that he capsized
the loom, which toppled over on to the road—a worm-
eaten heap of dust and rottenness! Ah! the black-
hearted, lying Canongate rascal. He wished him at that
moment no better fate than to be made to eat the dust
and bones of the battered loom, with all its living inhabitants.

It was a complete wreck, the beams having crumbled
down like pease meal, and the posts being so alive with
creeping things that he threw them all into the moss
at Silverburn.

" I went nae mair to yon toon to seek a loom, but got
a cannie, decent wright at Ninemileburn to make ane,
and wi' the lay and heddles and ither necessaries from
Biggar, I soon had the shuttle flying in a a'e-ended
house, and henceforward claimed the right to be ca'ed
a maister weaver in the Carlops." So the tale ended.

THE SCANDAL

It was the bairn that did it. The kirs'nin' o' wee
Jimmy, the seventh son of Tammas Broun, beadle in a
quiet Pentland parish, was an event of great importance
in every corner of the small community. Even the
youngster himself seemed to feel the importance of
being dressed so gaily in garments that he now saw
for the first time, but which had been before the pulpit
on six previous occasions.

The Rev. Mr. Riggs, the minister, was as bald as the
leather of his old pulpit Bible, but nobody knew that
save Tammas, who was precentor as well as beadle, and

ploughman, gardener, and orraman to the minister besides, and a stern, strict follower of his Covenanting forefathers. Every Sabbath morning Tammas had to see that the minister's wig sat straight upon his pow, but it was a duty that always filled his righteous soul with wrath—" the awdawcity o' a minister o' the Gospel preachin' frae the pulpit wi' siccan a lee on his heid! " So for that reason, and maybe a few others beside, there was little love lost between Tammas and the minister.

The sermon over, the mother brought in the child and took her place, the father coming forward to be addressed by the minister. To perform the ceremony Mr. Riggs, who was short in stature, came down a step or two of the pulpit stair to where the basin was, and Tammas, tall and stout, lifted the bairn out of his mother's lap, and held him up almost to the minister's nose. In deep silence the solemn words were spoken, but as soon as the water touched the child's face loud was his protest, and the father hastily turned to place the wean once more in the mother's lap. In doing so he failed to notice that one wicked little hand had clutched at and kept firm hold of a piece of narrow ribbon used in fixing the minister's wig; and so both wig and wean were safely deposited in the mother's arms.

Poor Mr. Riggs! The truth was out at last; and there he stood before the astonished congregation, wigless and bare-pow'd, till the father, vexed at such ungodly wark on the part of his bairn, yet unable exactly to keep down his inward satisfaction, handed him back the heathenish article, which the latter received with the whispered order, " Give out a psalm," and then retreated out of sight into the pulpit.

With serious face, the precentor asked the congregation to join in singing the last four verses of the seventh psalm, reading with slow and emphatic voice the words :

> " Upon his own head his mischief
>   shall be returned home ;
> His vi'lent dealing also down
>   On his own pate shall come."

The singing of the psalm gave the minister time to regain composure before appearing again to pronounce the benediction.   But after the kirk had skailed he came into the vestry, where his beadle was standing, and with angry face demanded, " Ay, man, what have ye to say for this day's wark ? letting that son o' Sawton scandaleeze the hale parish."

" I have jist this tae say, Mr. Riggs," said the father, " that though it may prove the doctrine o' original sin, it shows us hoo babes and sucklin's may be made instruments in the hands o' Providence for uncoverin' the shame o' the ungodly."

Needless to say, this unco ongoing at the " kirs'nin' " brought matters to a crisis, and poor Tammas found himself for a time among the unemployed.

THE STILL

Jamie was a weaver's apprentice.   After the day's work was done the weaver lads engaged in all sorts of recreations and pranks, and if it was not learning *The Gentle Shepherd* for the annual performance, it might be poaching or ferreting ; but one night Jamie and his friend Jake Scott had a fresh ploy in hand.   The district around the Carlops, Harlaw Moor, and Auchencorth Moss hid many a still, and it was reported that " sma' stills " were as common as snuff-boxes. Nearly every farm had some place where a still was working, and at the kitchen fire in not a few private houses stills were kept going every winter. One weaver with a ready market for his product at eighteen shillings a gallon found it so profitable that he gave up weaving altogether. But stills of this kind were never so popular as those situated in lonely spots among the hills, in far-away cleughs or old quarries with water running near by.

Jamie knew that his friend Dod the Dyker had a still that he often moved from one place to another so as to minimize the risk of detection. He was then working it in a sequestered hollow, a wild and windy place shut out from the world, called the Windy Gowl. Dod's partner was Jake Scott's father, Willie Scott, the smith at South Mains, and it was arranged that Jamie and Jake should lend a hand next night.

The apparatus consisted of an ordinary boiler, in which was boiled the " maut " or broken barley out of which the spirit was made. A pipe led from the top of the boiler down through a barrel of cold water, the part in the barrel being shaped like a corkscrew, till it got to the bottom, where it protruded an inch or two. Through this pipe came the whisky in the form of steam, to be cooled by the water in the barrel. A receptacle under the barrel caught the liquid as it dribbled from the worm. In order that the pipe, or worm, should be kept cool, the water required to be frequently changed, and the assistance of the lads was accordingly welcomed by the men.

As can be imagined, the practised hands did not all

sit there complacently for hours while this was taking place without refreshing themselves with what was a different spirit from that which now passes under the name of whisky ; and while seated round the fire listening to a poaching story that was being told by Dod, up jumped Jake Scott and cried " Wheest."

Jamie nearly fell to the ground with fright, for that night there was in the Gowl a darkness and a silence that could be felt and made you hold your breath in fear.

" What did ye hear, Jake ? " eagerly whispered his father.

" Somebody speakin'," he answered softly, whereupon Dod cocked his head to one side, and heard distinctly sounds as of some dry sticks breaking among the bushes.

" The gaugers ! " he muttered, " an' if they're man for man we'll fecht them."

" They're no worth the fechtin'," said Willie Scott, " but never a drap o' this precious spirit will they get," and suiting the action to the sentiment he gave the keg, half full of spirits, a push with his foot that sent it rolling into the burn.

By this time Jamie was trembling all over, fervently wishing he was at home. There was no time for delay. He saw the others standing with their sticks ready to strike ; but for him standing was out of the question, so he scrambled up the slope on the other side of the burn and in mounting over a dry-stane dyke he tumbled head over heels.

As he gathered himself together he saw an awesome sight. Out of the long grass and bracken there rose up before him a figure like a man, and he saw clear between him and the sky a pair of horns on the head ! Then he heard voices. On their coming nearer, the figure with the horns moved away, and he recognized the voices to be those of the herd and the ploughman at South Mains, who had been away seeing their sweethearts at Carlops Farm, and were much astonished at seeing Jamie rising up from among the bracken.

" Where's he gane ? " inquired Jamie, looking round in amazement and terror.

" Where's what gane ? " they speired, and Jamie told them what he had seen.

" Od, man," said the herd, " oor cattle beasts are feedin' here the noo ; I'se warrant 'ee it's been ane of them 'ee tumbled ower. I noticed they were a' lyin' doon, and ane rose up when 'oo cam' forrit."

" That's jaist been it," solemnly added the ploughman ; " it wad be ane o' the Gal'ways wi' the muckle horns ; it wad be risin' whan 'ee saw it, an' 'ee thocht it was the de'il, did 'ee ? haw ! haw ! haw ! "

Gal'ways or no Gal'ways, that dark night's work with evil spirits in the Windy Gowl, with its stills and worms and smuggled kegs, was like a nightmare to Jamie. He hurried home to bed and covered his head in the blankets, wishful to forget it all, for falling into the hands of the gaugers was the fate that the apprentices feared most. And it comforted him to learn afterwards that all the paraphernalia had at last fallen into the hands of the gaugers, and that the dyker and the smith had got such an " awfu' fleg " that they never started another still in the Pentlands.

Chapter XX

LINTON STORIES

The Whipman Play

" Whipman Play " Societies were common in every town and village in the Lothians in the early part of the nineteenth century, and during the last few years, with the revival of all kinds of ancient customs, folk-lore, pageants, and processions, the Whipman Play has been resuscitated in many country villages to the delight of every one—old and young, native and visitor alike.

" The Whipmen of Linton Society " was first instituted in 1803 as a Benevolent Society. Under its auspices there is now held a summer festival in which all sections of the community combine to make a happy holiday.

The summer day on which the play was held long ago was one of great interest to all in the surrounding countryside—farmers and farriers, herds and hillmen, cobblers and carriers, weavers and woodmen. There was keen rivalry. Horses were decorated with ribbons, wisps of straw and cunningly devised ornaments, and by dint of unwearied expenditure of elbow-grease in cleaning and polishing harness all was made to shine and glitter for the occasion. The lads with blue bonnets and braw new breeches, and with penny canes for riding switches, were gazed upon with awe and admiration by all the villagers, especially by the lasses.

A story is told of an early representation of the play—just over a hundred years ago—from which it is learned that the members gathered on the Green and rode to the president's house, where a procession was formed to visit all the important houses in the parish, returning to the Green, where the real fun began. Here the races were held. Ritchie, the teller of the tale, narrates how his father had objected to his taking part in the races, as he wished neither to have his master's horse foundered nor his son's neck broken. But the temptation could not be resisted—were not the prizes a lure in themselves: horse brechames, saddles, whips, lamps, everything down to twopence worth of whipcord?

The course was a mile in the Broomlee direction and back again. Unfortunately he failed to get a good start, and brought up the rear during the whole race, but succeeded in knocking down the man who was doing duty as the turning-post.

The dinner in the old Linton Inn was the chief event after the races. On this occasion, however, a mishap occurred to our friend which rather daunted his spirits. All who came from a distance stabled their horses at the inn, and after the dinner each went to find his horse and mount for home. It happened that the innkeeper's daughter had been receiving particular attention from Ritchie during the day, and he determined that when she came to the door to see him off he would give her a splendid salute, just to let her see how well he could emulate the laird, who was noted for the manner of his salute.

One after another was helped into his saddle, but

Ritchie disdained any help, and putting his foot in the stirrup, and gripping saddle and mane, stood ready to mount. His horse had a bad habit of moving off whenever he felt the reins in the hand or the foot in the stirrup, which sometimes made the mounting difficult ; and knowing well this habit he decided to make such an effort as would land him safely in the saddle. Accordingly he made the spring, just at the moment when he caught the eye of his loved one beaming upon him from the door. He rose, he says, like a laverock on the wing, graceful and easy, reaching the saddle and no mistake, when, heigh presto ! he overshot the mark and went head first over the other side into the watering trough that stood at the inn door.

Every one roared with laughter, but poor Ritchie fancied he heard the laughter of the innkeeper's daughter above that of all the others, so picking himself up out of the trough, his braw buckskins dripping wet, he slipped away as quietly as he could. The day had ended badly for Ritchie ; the light and jocund heart of half an hour ago was cast down and desolate ; but saddest of all, his hope of winning the affection of the lass at the inn was blighted for ever.

To-day also there is much ceremonial and circumambulation, joined with mirth and merriment in the gladsome festival, in which five parishes participate—Newlands, Dunsyre, Kirkurd, Dolphinton, and Linton—and careful and painstaking preparations are made to ensure its success. Whoever has looked upon this scene of rejoicing on the village Green in its setting of peculiar natural beauty, gay with many-coloured costumes of processionists and participants in tableaux and pageantry, tense with rivalry in music, sport, and dancing, resplendent in the sunshine and beauty of midsummer, cherishes a memory of rural happiness and pure delight that gladdens the heart. "Sweet Auburn," with all its mirth, was never more happy than Linton on the Play Day.

A Trial for Poaching

There was a time in the history of West Linton when a court was held twice a year, before the Whitsunday and Martinmas terms. This Justice of the Peace Court tried such cases as debt recovery, actions for damages, and poaching. Poaching cases were also tried at Noble-house by J.P.'s specially summoned for the purpose, but the Linton Court was a regularly constituted institution. All those cases became the common talk of the country-side, and every one who had the slightest interest in them, or wanted amusement at the expense of some one else, attended the court.

All the Linton boys and girls got a holiday on court days, for the court was held in the school near the Cross, the schoolmaster acting as clerk of court. A hush fell upon the audience as with solemnity the justices filed in, headed by the chief constable of Linton with red coat and cocked hat. Among the justices were the Lairds of Halmyre, Broomlee, and Macbiehill, and the minister, Mr. Forrester, along with a Major Grahame, who was as hard on poachers as his forebear was on Covenanters.

Almost every case had some point of humour. A ploughman, Rob Donald, summoned Tom Tweedie, a tailor, for the misfit of a pair of trousers, and claimed 7s. 6d. damages. Rob gave his evidence and stated how he had trysted Tom Tweedie to come to West Mains to do the work, promising to pay him the usual tailor's fee of eighteenpence a day and his meals ; that he had made a misfit, thereby spoiling the material and putting him to expense, for which he now claimed damages.

" What did you say was wrong with the breeks ? " inquired one of the justices.

" They were misfitted, sir."

" Oh ! where about ? "

" Oo, a' ways ; he made them wi' a lang leg an' a short ane, forbye puttin' ower muckle claith intae anither pairt."

" And where was this other part ? " asked the chairman ; but Rob hesitated.

" In what neighbourhood ? " insisted another laird.

" Weel, if ye maun ken, it was in the hinner end." This caused great merriment, and Rob was told to resume his seat.

It was now Tom Tweedie's turn.

" You made a pair of breeks, Tom, for Rob Donald ? "

" Ay, brawly I ken that, sir. I made a pair for yer lordship tae a while syne."

" Well, never mind that just now. Is it true that you made one leg shorter than the other ? "

" Na, na, deevil a fear o' me daein' that ; but maybe ane was longer than the other."

On being further questioned about " the other part " he replied that he wanted to return good for evil, and gave good measure for the small allowance of meat and drink that had been given to him.

He promised to remedy the defect if the court would let him off, and this was agreed to.

WATCHING SHEEP-DOG TRIALS, WEST LINTON.

Another case concerned Sandy M'Nab, a farmer in Carlops, who was summoned by the schoolmaster for damage done to his cabbages by Sandy's kye, and the sum of 5s. was claimed.

The farmer denied liability, and said that the schoolmaster's fence round the kailyard was insufficient for its purpose, but the latter asserted the paling was a good one until the kye broke it down. No witnesses were brought, and the justices were in a quandary. In such cases reference was usually made to the minister. He suggested that perhaps some one could speak as to this fence.

At last a weaver came forward, and was asked if he thought the fence good enough for what it was intended.

" Yes," he said ; " it was an ordinar' palin'."

" Strong enough to keep out a cow, do you think ? "

" Yes, if she was a reasonable beast."

" Do you know anything about Sandy's kye ? "

" Weel, no ; but I've heard they were just geyan like his-sel."

After further consideration, the verdict was awarded in favour of the schoolmaster, but as only ten cabbages had been eaten, 3s. 6d. was thought to be sufficient recompense.

It was the " Poachin' Case," however, that excited the greatest interest, and most of the Carlops weavers had made the occasion a holiday, and had come to Linton Court to hear it and to enjoy the fun.

Among the weavers poaching with the gun and shooting at Raffles on Hansel Mondays, Whipman Plays, and Hallowe'ens were among the chief amusements. Sandy Cameron had never learned to shoot, and so had never been able to compete for the prizes that were so much coveted—a fat sow, a gallon or two of whisky, and several cheeses. He determined to remedy this ; so he borrowed a gun from Simon Cook, one of the two Carlops constables, and made his way one evening to the Hooley Haugh in Habbie's How to begin his practice.

Two apprentice weavers—Willie Tod and Tom Kirkhope—saw him go, and scented a ploy. One of them was bringing home a hare tied up in a handkerchief, which he took care to hide from Sandy, and the three of them walked together to the Haugh. Willie offered to load the gun, and in sheer devilment rammed down a double charge of powder and handed it back to the trembling Sandy. Arriving in the Haugh, Sandy brought the gun up to his shoulder, closed his eyes, and fired. When the smoke cleared, only his feet were to be seen—the " kick " had knocked him over into the burn behind him. Willie was quick to take advantage of this, and whipping out the hare he ran off in the direction the gun had pointed, and cried out as he stopped and held up the hare, " Capital, Sandy, capital ; 'ee've shot a hare, a thumpin' hare ! "

By this time Sandy had got up out of the burn, shivering with fright, but he beamed when he saw the hare and ran forward as if to embrace it. Then with evident satisfaction he put it into the neuk of his plaid ; and Willie's face fell, for he was afraid he was to be the loser by his prank.

Then the unfortunate thing happened. Randie Ross, the other Carlops constable, had a grudge against his brother constable Simon, who had lent the gun, and he stepped out in front of them and demanded of Sandy what he had under his plaid.

" Oo, jist Simon's gun, that I had doon at the Haugh

practeesin' for the Raffles next week," replied Sandy, feeling somewhat uncomfortable.

" Jist tell me nae mair lees, but deliver up the hare at aince, for I was watchin' a' the time." Sandy turned pale.

" Ah, ha ! found trespassin', wi' a gun, on the lands o' Newha', and a hare found in possession ; a fine job for ye gien Friday, Sandy," said the constable, as he lifted up the hare. " A braw beast, tae, an' it'll keep fine till the court day, when the justices 'll a' see't for themselves," he added with a chuckle.

Randie had seen the gun sticking out of Sandy's plaid, and had followed unseen, but had not been sufficiently near to see how the hare had been obtained.

Sandy declared that when he fired he saw no hare, and couldn't shoot a hare even if he did see one ; nevertheless he was summoned to appear at the Linton Court.

There the case was duly called, and there were many serious faces in court when it was seen that Major Grahame was present, for he was the dread of all poachers.

The only witness against Sandy was the constable—and the hare. He gave a full description of the whole matter so far as he knew it, and concluded by saying how, at the risk of his life, he had confronted Sandy, and taken the hare from him.

" Have you anything to say before we pass sentence ? " demanded the chairman ; but the irascible major intervened, " Oh, fine him at once ; fine him at once, and be done with it."

But Sandy implored them to wait a minute, for he had witnesses to prove it wasn't true—Willie Tod and

Tom Kirkhope. These two lads had promised Sandy that they would do anything to get him off.

Willie's interrogation came first. He denied that he had seen Sandy M'Nab shoot a hare, or fire at one, or that a hare had been found in his possession.

" Then you make out that Constable Randie Ross here is telling a falsehood ? " observed one of the justices, to which Willie replied that this was " naething by-ordinar' tae them that kens him."

This irritated the major, who ejaculated, " Just fine him too ! "

Willie got a fright when he saw Randie fumbling at his plaid, and thought he was going to produce the hare, and prove the witnesses to be perjurers.

It was now Tom's turn to be questioned, and he made the same replies as his friend. A stillness fell upon the court as the chairman pointed out that both witnesses had flatly contradicted Constable Randie's statement that a hare was found in Cameron's possession, and he was upon the point of asking that the hare be brought in, when the minister rose and asked if it would not be better to hear if any of his brother constables could speak regarding the matter, and as to his character as a truthful witness, before taking in the hare as evidence.

Simon Cook was accordingly called, and replied that Randie Ross and he were constables in the Carlops, and that he " had no doubt his intentions in this case were honest enough."

" You don't mean to say it's a case of mistaken identity ? " put in one of the justices, to which Cook replied, " I didna mean to say onything, but I ken that my freend Randie there is that blind as no tae ken a bee frae a bat."

This annoyed Randie ; his red hair bristled and his eyes shone. "Ay, maybe ay, an' maybe no, Maister Cook, but I can tell a guid fat hare when I see't." Whereupon, suiting the action to the word, he came forward to the table with the handkerchief, which he loosened, when out tumbled upon the floor—a puppy dog !

Consternation and confusion reigned—the schoolroom was in an uproar, but Randie was sore perplexed.

The change had been effected when Randie's plaid was hanging in the schoolroom, and the lads had whispered to Simon what they had done.

The case was found " Not proven," and one of the justices, with a twinkle in his eye, told Randie he could have the hare home with him for his trouble.

Great applause followed, showing how much satisfaction the acquittal had given to all, and not least to the Carlops weavers.

Needless to say, however, that Hallowe'en passed without any attempt being made by Sandy Cameron to win the coveted prizes.

" At Dead o' Night "

The adventures of those who watched graveyards in bygone days, in order to counteract the depredations of body-snatchers, form the subject of many stories. A tale is told of Linton Kirkyard, where one cold winter night Willie Winks and Johnny Bald took their turn at watching. Stories had been rife in the district that more than one " liftin' " had been successfully carried out. Then there were the Burke and Hare stories

from Edinburgh, Currie, and other places, that had struck fear and terror into many hearts.

Night arrived, and Willie, a decent weaver body, left home with the usual supply of food and refreshment to meet Johnny at the Bridge. Johnny was in good spirits, and this had a salutary effect on Willie, who became less doleful, notwithstanding the thought of the nine hours ahead of him.

Johnny was a little deaf, and this had led to his being discharged from the army; but he was a cheery man, with a great fund of stories of his soldiering days, and was now a blacksmith to trade, with an army pension. That night he brought a bayonet with him, in case, as he said, there might be a skirmish, and there was a gun in the watch-house.

In those days Linton Kirkyard was almost square, bounded on one side by the Green, the gate being on that side facing the Lyne. Near by stood the watch-house, having a window looking into the kirkyard.

The beadle arrived about the same time as the watchers, just to see them take up their duties. All sat quietly together for a while telling stories, and then, after cautioning them to keep a good fire burning and pointing out where the powder and shot were kept, the old beadle said "Good-night," and hirpled away on his stick into the darkness, as the wild wind from the Cauldstaneslap soughed down through the trees and among the tombstones.

From above the fireplace Johnny took down the gun and examined it with the trained eye of a soldier. This heartened Willie, although he heard a noise at the gate, but it was only caused by two Linton lads who were in a mood to have a crack. When they left, it was approaching the dead hour of night when kirkyards yawn, and with the candle spluttering, and shadows dancing at the open door, and the darkness of the kirkyard beyond, Willie was beginning to feel the effects of the eeriness. To keep him from thinking about it all he began to whistle some Scottish airs—"Blue Bonnets over the Border," "Scots wha hae," and "Wha widna fecht for Charlie."

Johnny inquired what tune it was he was whistling, and on being told it was "Wha widna fecht . . ." he replied, "Ay, did ye ever fecht, Willie? Ye ken—when I was in the army . . ."

Willie started another tune, and asked Johnny how he liked it, for he was wanting to keep off fighting, bayonets, guns, and such like. But Johnny never heeded, for when once he was started on his battles there was no stopping him.

"I mind once spearing a nigger—ay, wi' this same bayonet," but Willie whistled louder to keep up his spirits.

"I'll tell you an adventure I had with a ghost in the Peninsular War," continued Johnny. But Willie kept on whistling, for at the mention of ghosts his nerves were like to get the better of him.

"Stop whistling," cried Johnny. "Don't you know that's just an invitation to ghosts? But there's maybe worse than ghosts abroad this night," he continued. "Did you hear about that affair at Newbattle the other night?"

"No," said Willie, looking over his shoulder at the door, "but you can tell me about it some other time." And still wanting to change the subject, Willie con-

tinued, " Do you think we'll have some curlin' this
winter ? "

" Man," replied Johnny, " it's awfu' hoo things are
gaun enoo. At Pentland, they say, there's nothing in
the kirkyard but empty coffins, and at Penicuik——"

" Did ye hear that ? " cried Willie, as a sound of
something moving in the kirkyard came to his ear, and
he moved nearer to the fire.

" Ye silly carl, am I not telling ye this very minute
what I heard," said Johnny, not understanding in his
deafness what Willie had meant.—" Hoo that at Penicuik they're thinking there's body-liftin' gaun on in
spite o' their watchin', for a gig passed Brigend the
ither nicht in the deid hours wi' three folk in it, but the
middle ane sitting so straucht and stiff that naebody had
the least doubt. Ay, and at Glencorse——"

" There it is again," cried Willie, as he thought he
heard this time the sound of a pick or a shovel. " Oh,
Johnny, take up the gun and look to the primin'."

But nothing would stop Johnny in his story.—" And
then the Newbattle business—the watchers saw them
at their work and chased them, firing at one just as he
was getting over a dyke ; they didn't catch any of
them, but there was a trail of blood seen afterwards all
the way to Stobshill."

" Oh, murder," gasped Willie, " they're coming this
way," and sure enough they were, for Johnny, despite
all his deafness, had heard the sound and, seizing hold
of the gun, faced the door, while Willie picked up the
bayonet and stood behind him.

It was a trying moment for poor Willie, whose heart
was thudding against his ribs, his legs trembling, and
his knees knocking.

WEST LINTON FROM CASTLELAW.

" Put the candle in the lantern and we'll gang an' see, for they're no comin' ony nearer," cried the brave Johnny.

Willie did as he was told, and then went forward to the door, though he would rather have stayed in the bield of the watch-house. A heavy step was heard on the footpath, then on the turf. " We'll hae tae warn them afore we fire—three times," said Johnny, adding in a low voice, " Who goes there ? "

There was no answer, and the noise stopped. " Who goes there ? " Still no answer.

" Who goes there ? " repeated Johnny for the third time in a voice loud enough to awaken the dead. Still there was no answer ; but the noise was heard again.

It came nearer. Willie's lantern shone about ten yards in front, past the side of Johnny's head, but he dared not look in front. By this time the hand holding the bayonet was also holding on to Johnny's coat tail. His hair was on end, and just as he caught sight of the legs of two resurrectionists coming into the light of the lantern, Johnny fired !

And the noise ! Johnny was brave, but he wasn't prepared for a noise like that, so he took to his heels and ran. Willie followed, dropping the lantern, but still holding on to the coat tail. Then Johnny tripped on a gravestone, and both fell headlong on the turf.

Terrified, they lay for a moment. When they came to themselves, they saw somebody approaching with a lantern. It was the old beadle ; and the next minute they both welcomed him. He had heard the report of the gun and came to learn the cause of it, and it was only when he said he would stay the rest of the night with them that they agreed to continue the watch.

As may be surmised, the beadle wanted to hear all about the affair, and set out to see if there had been any black work done that night, so, leaving Johnny and Willie in the watch-house, he went off with his lantern to survey the kirkyard.

When he came back he seemed troubled and thoughtful and very quiet, then sitting down on a form, and giving his head a scratch, he said in his own slow, moralizing style, " Ay, man, but I'm sorry ; it was stipid o' me, though, rale stipid—sheer idiocy in fact. Pair Sandy Gifford's cuddy ! Ye see, I forgot to steek the yett, and he got into the kirkyard frae the Green, and was quietly wanderin' aboot amang the stanes nibblin' the fine sweet grass that grows there. Ay, it was rale stipid, but I'm thankfu' he's no deid, he's jist lame ! " and then he whispered confidentially, " Bit never let daub ! "

And no one ever " let daub " till long afterwards ; but not a few of the Linton worthies wondered how Sandy's cuddy had got so stiff, never dreaming for a moment that its four legs had got the charge of shot that had been intended for the legs of a pair of body-snatchers in Linton Kirkyard at deid o' nicht.

"THE LAST DAY!"

Sandy came to see me the other day.   " Man," says he, " it's the last day ! "

" The last day for what ? " I inquired.

" The last day for the fishin', of course," says he petulantly.

Now Sandy comes from the West Highlands, and few

are the West Highland streams and hill burns out of which he has not taken hundreds of trout in his time; but the season had been a poor one—in fact, it made one forget about "the last day" altogether. But Sandy's Highland heart was stirred. In the city's autumn sunshine he saw the hills and the blue sky, the sunlit, foam-flecked water tumbling down the hill burn, making ideal pools for fishing, and a lusty trout on his line; he saw himself fishing till the darkness came down—the darkness of the last day—with trout in his basket, and in his heart the joy and the quiet peace of happiness that only the fisher knows.

So it was agreed that on this short Saturday afternoon we should fish a certain Pentland burn.

Sandy set off in high glee up the stream, and soon he was in his glory killing trout. Ay, they were small, but what of that? They seemed to know it was the last day, playing high jinks up and down the burn. I think Sandy could have made as much speed guddlin' as with the rod; still, he was doing well; and, catching fish or not, it was a delight to be here among the hills and moorlands, to smell the wet moss, the earth, and the grass, to catch a glimpse of the dippers, dainty little fellows in evening dress, so polite, skimming about up and down stream.

There was also a kestrel hunting, and some carrion crows; otherwise, Nature was still. The autumn peace was over everything; the hillsides that artists have often painted were a study in every hue of brown, and the undertone of sweet, refreshing melody came from the merry stream.

It was after five; the glen was shut out from the sun; it grew colder and darker, but we could not get Sandy off the water. Running out from the shepherd's cottage, past which the stream flowed, I shouted to Sandy that the tea was ready, and the table groaning beneath the load of every variety of scones.

" But," says Sandy, cunningly, " I'm just changing my cast. I'm getting in among them now. I feel I'm going to get a big basket."

Alas! he was defeated by the darkness, and in due time he appeared with blinking eyes in the lamplight of the cottage kitchen.

" I've had a grand day," he said. " I'm sorry the fishin's done for another year; but, oh, the spring'll soon be here again, and I mean to make an early start."

Dear old Sandy, nearly three score years and ten, with his white hair and red chubby cheeks! What a buoyant, hopeful young heart is his, filled with the utmost joy and serenity in all the greatest things in life—the simplest and most natural. The fact that he had been on the water and had cast many a line, that he had heard the cries of the hill birds and the rippling of the burn, had brought supreme satisfaction, quite apart from the fish that lay in his basket.

The tea, accompanied by the talk about sheep and dogs, the show and the trials, the visits of the minister and the laird, and all the gossip of the glen, was a feast for all who love country ways; and Sandy had his own stories. Like the successful fisher in the *Noctes* he knew what it was to have " creel fou, pouches fou, and a lot o' great muckle anes hangin' on a string." And very seldom could he voice " The Angler's Complaint " with any justification, for he could catch fish when no other could get " a bite "—

MENDICK HILL.

Sometimes ower early,
Sometimes ower late,
Sometimes nae water,
Sometimes a spate,
Sometimes ower calm,
Sometimes ower clear,
There's aye something wrang
When I'm fishin' here."

"Peep o' Day"

Peep o' Day was a faithful servant, always diligent about his master's business. Summer and winter he was out and about the farm long before any one else, and no matter at what hour the farmer appeared Peep o' Day was ready to accompany him on his round of inspection. His master was one of that rare old type of gentleman farmers who requested rather than ordered his servants to do a certain thing, and spoke in a soft, musical voice, slowly, kindly, interestedly. He was, however, quite unaware of Peep o' Day's one failing.

Peep was a poacher, and for a long time Peter, the gamekeeper, had been keeping an eye upon him, and only waited his opportunity to pounce upon him. There was therefore no love lost between the two. Peter had frequently been outwitted, and he resolved to get the better of Peep. But Peep was on good terms with the early morning hours; often they had sheltered him from discovery and always they had served him well, while Peter was more to be dreaded in the evening hours than at the break o' day.

On one occasion Peep was nearly caught. He had set a trap close to a rabbit run on the side of a wood on his master's property, but the pin was fixed outside the boundary. Bunny was duly caught, but was still alive when the keeper arrived and discovered Peep hiding near by. An altercation ensued in which Peep maintained that the rabbit was his, that the trap was set outside Peter's province, and that Peter had nothing to do with it.

"Well," said Peter, "I can no more allow you to tether rabbits on my ground than to poach them, and the rabbit's mine." So Peep allowed him to have his way, and was glad to escape.

But at last the day of reckoning came. Peep had been fairly caught, and was led in triumph by the keeper back to the farmyard, and brought before the master, to whom he related the story of his capture. Peep had been poaching and was caught in the act, and here was the brown hare.

The good-natured master turned to Peep and softly inquired, "And what were you going to do with the hare, Edward?"

Edward, *alias* Peep, very crestfallenly replied, "I was going to sell it, sir."

"You were going to sell it, Edward?"

"Yes, sir."

"Well, Edward, I will buy it from you."

Peter turned pale, then flushed crimson. Peep was paid for the brown hare, and his master took him afresh to his bosom, for he loved his servant as a brother, to whom he had given the happy soubriquet of "Peep o' Day."

Chapter XXI

DOLPHINTON YARNS

FOR the Hill-walker who thirsts for further knowledge of his Hills of Home, there is a delightful land in the wild places of moor, hill, and stream above and around Dunsyre and Dolphinton. The latter place is little more than an hour's run by bus from Edinburgh by way of the Carlops and West Linton, and is a good starting-point for the Covenanter's Grave, the Ravens' Cleuch, and the Garval Syke by way of the Medwin Valley, and for the various crossings by right-of-way to Harburn and Auchengray, Carnwath, and the Crane Loch.

At Medwinhead a well-marked drove road goes through the moors to Slipperfield Farm and Linton. From Fernyhaugh Farm another right-of-way, which passes the large cairns called the Nether and Upper Cairns and the Rumbling Well, goes to join the drove road already mentioned at a point in the valley between Slipperfield Mount and Mendick Hill. These unfrequented hill walks will in time become better known to Pentland Walkers in search of pastures new; and with the present facility of reaching a convenient starting-point the district will come to be discovered as a land abounding in all the joys and surprises that are the delight of Hill-walkers. With Bartholomew's Map for Pedestrians as guide, no difficulty will be experienced in finding these less-known rights-of-way.

The pleasure of a day's ramble is not measured by the number of miles we cover, and a walk becomes an adventure when we are unaware of how or where it is going to terminate. On one occasion I set out from Dolphinton for a day upon the hills, accompanied by a native of the district who was well versed in all its lore of story and antiquity, but we got no farther than the top of the Black Mount, and there, lying among the heather on a warm summer day, he unfolded to me some of the stories of the district that lay stretched like a map in the wide valley beneath us.

It is a countryside that did not escape the attention of the Border raiders, for there were drove roads from the North that passed through the parish, and many an encounter took place in which blood was spilt and sheep and cattle carried off.

In the strath between Hell's Cleuch and the Pentland heights a stillness lies over the drove roads in the night time, and there is an uncanniness in the black darkness when the winds are roving. In fancy we can hear the jingle of spurs and bridle and the thudding of horses' hoofs as the raiders went over the heather tracks on desperate errands, for they rode " in the rain and the wind and the lave."

Near the point at Melbourne where the Dolphinton–Biggar road is bisected by the Elsrickle–Peebles road there once stood an old inn or " Yull-hoose " called Lochhead. It was much frequented by drovers, and was probably one of those places where, on payment of a small fee, the wayworn animals with their keepers might rest for the night. Among these men were some

MEDWINHEAD.

who were rough and uncouth, and the local story is
told that one night a party of noisy drovers came along
and demanded supper in terms that were justly resented
by the sturdy serving woman, who, with sleeves rolled
up, attended upon them. Yes, it was brose they wanted,
with a plentiful supply of buttermilk, and soon the
hungry cattlemen began to devour their meal. But
they found that there appeared to be an unusual number
of hairs in the milk, and were not slow to call the attention of the woman to the fact. Whereupon she turned
to the barrel, and with a swoop of her arm dived into
the milk and pulled forth—a drowned cat.

An unsavoury story of wild men. But the buxom
wench exulted in the triumph of her revenge, and was
not slow to spread the news around the countryside,
which accounts for the story being still current to-day,
although the house in which the scene was enacted has
long since disappeared.

Although many of the lairds in the Pentland area were
Jacobites and took part in the " Risings," there were
Loyalists also among the inhabitants. George Ferguson,
of Dolphinton, was one of these ; a strong young man
of twenty-five, mighty in valour, powerful in muscle,
with a great shock of red hair, who, hearing of the doings
of the Chevalier, determined to offer his services to the
King. He mounted his horse, and rode to Falkirk and
presented himself for enlistment. But the King's officer
who questioned Ferguson must have been a poor judge
of men.

" You have no training ? And your horse has probably never been off the road ? "

" No."

" Well, then, you had better go back to your home,

but as a token of your devotion and loyalty to His Majesty I present you with this sword."

Ferguson returned home crestfallen, but proud of his sword, which remained a treasured possession in his family long after he had been laid to rest in Dowfinton Kirkyard.

Major Learmonth, the Laird of Newholm, near Dunsyre, who commanded the Covenanters' horse at Rullion Green in 1666, is also buried there. During the battle his horse was shot under him, and he fell, but stepping back a little to a fold-dyke, he killed one of the four horsemen who pursued him, mounted his horse, and came safe off from the other three.

Thirteen years later he was in charge of a body of horse and foot that came from Tweeddale and took part in the Battle of Bothwell Bridge (June 22, 1679), and afterwards hid from his pursuers in an underground room at Newholm, to which entrance was obtained from the banks of the Medwin. Although he was at length caught and ordered for execution, the sentence was commuted to one of imprisonment in the Bass. He survived the Revolution, however, and died at Newholm in 1693, in his eighty-eighth year, an elder of Dolphinton Kirk. The church is one of the smallest in Scotland, but many notable ministers have laboured there since John de St. Andrews was rector in 1253.

He was a jovial minister of Dolphinton of whom this story is told. A neighbouring minister had written a pamphlet upon the subject of " Joseph and his Brethren" which was sold at a local store conducted by a Willie Noble ; but, not meeting with the expected demand, the pamphlet was reduced in price to ninepence. Our merry friend, wishing to retaliate upon his neighbour for some hard knock which had been administered by him at an earlier period, used the opportunity in the following manner :

The local school at Knocknowes was to be examined in Bible knowledge. This duty was to be performed by the Dolphinton minister, and as he was making his way across country to the examination he passed a boy whom he knew, and asked him where he was going, seeing that the lad was dressed in his Sunday suit.

" Oh," replied the boy, " this is our examination day."

" Yes," said the minister, " and I'm going to examine you in Bible knowledge. Now, if I were to ask you ' Who sold Joseph,' what would you reply ? "

" His brethren, sir."

" Quite right. Quite right. And if I asked you ' For how much did they sell him,' what would you answer ? "

" For thirty pieces of silver, sir."

Then the minister, fond of a joke, and wishing to pay off the old score against his brother, prompted the boy how he was to reply when these questions were put, and the result was that when the class was asked " Who sold Joseph ? " the answer came, " Willie Noble, sir," and " For how much ? "—" Please sir, for ninepence ! "

" Ay," commented my old friend, " they're just human beings like oorsel's they ministers, and some o' them has sair failings ; ay, bitter, bitter some o' them can be, but I often think they had mair sense o' humour in the auld days, and were fonder o' a joke than they are now—but times are serious, o' ay, verra serious, nae doubt, nae doubt. Weel, weel, it's a guid thing aye to be learnin'. Look ye," said he, " that auld plane tree at the corner o' the Kirk Road yonder was brought as a saplin' frae Craigmillar in the year o' the Forty-five.

And it was along that very road in the same year," he continued confidentially, " so they say, that some of Prince Charlie's men went up by Newbigging and Kaimend to Mr. Lockhart's house at Carnwath for horses which he had provided for them to take with them to England."

There was great confusion in Carnwath that day, for it was the Sabbath, and the folks were all sitting quietly in the kirk, when suddenly the door was thrown open and a stentorian voice announced, " The rebels are coming ! The rebels are coming ! "

" Weel, my friends," said the minister, " let us implore the Divine protection before we separate," and in the course of his prayer included the petition that the Lord would put " hooks on their noses, and bridles in their jaws, and turn them back by the way that they came."

Having obtained the horses from the young laird, the Highlanders departed, but " Libberton congregation broke up in great alarm on account of the rebels being at Carnwath, so that no collection was made for the poor."

There was many a coming and going at Carnwath, openly and secretly, in the days of the Old and the Young Chevalier, when the Lockharts were living at the " big house " there.

My companion did not confine himself entirely to historic yarns.

" Look again ! " he said, and pointed over the valley to a fir wood, where there is a milestone that marks the boundary of Peeblesshire and Lanarkshire. " There's a camping ground that's been used from time out of mind by the gipsies, and a bit beyond it yonder is the site of the old tollhouse of Harestanes "—probably from Har-

stane, Cymric for a boundary stone—" where there's
what some call a Druid Circle."

This consists of a setting of five stones in the garden
forming an irregular oval, 18 feet by 11 feet. The
largest stone is 4 feet 6 inches high, 3 feet 4 inches
broad, and 2 feet 4 inches thick. They are of local
volcanic rock, one being of vesicular basalt, which in all
likelihood was borne by the ice from the Western Pentlands, and a small flagstone occupying the centre of the
circle is probably the cap stone of a cist.

" It is curious how such a circle of stones came to
be there," he remarked ; " it must have had some significance, and no doubt there's some story about it in
the ancient history of this wonderful countryside."

Names such as Chesters, Keir Camp, and Carmaben
in the district point to Roman occupation, and the story
of the camp on the Lyne, not very far away, is well
known.

" Ye'll hae heard Dr. John Brown's story of the
Biggar minister's pig ? " he inquired, and without waiting for my reply he began the story :

" The minister of Biggar wished to send a present of
one of his pedigreed pigs to his brother minister and
friend in Dolphinton, and Rob Forsyth, the minister's
man, was entrusted with the errand. He was specially
enjoined to give a full account of the genealogy of the
porker.

" ' And ye see, Rob, be sure ye tell this afore ye let it
out o' the poke, for he'll never heed a word ye say after
that for glowerin' at its perfections.'

" Rob got the length of Candyburn Inn, and here he
met his old friend Ritchie, a humorist and wag.

" ' Whaur are ye gaun ? ' inquired Ritchie.

" ' Oo, I'm gaun tae Dowfintoun wi' joost the wunner-fu'st pig ever was piggit ; it's for the minister.'

" ' Ay, man, come yer ways in and tak' a dram, an' let's see the pig.'

" The pig was duly seen and admired, and they had a crack, and then, unknown to Rob, Ritchie substituted a young puppy dog for the pig; and off Rob trudged to the manse of Dowfinton.

" ' What's this in the poke, Rob, my man ? ' asks the minister on meeting him.

" ' Ay, ye may weel speir, Mr. Meek. It's just the maist extraordnar pig ever was. My master has sent it as a parteekler present to you, wi' his compliments.'

" ' Let's see't, Rob.'

" ' Na, na, sir, I maun first enlighten you as to its pedigree,' and as he proceeded to detail its antecedents it fell out at the corner of the poke. Up jumped the puppy winking and lively.

" ' That's a dowg, Rob,' says the minister.

" ' A dowg ! A dowg ! as shur's daith it is a dowg; it was—as shure, Mr. Meek—as fac's daith—it was a pig whan it gaed in ! '

" ' Weel, Rob, it's a dowg now, so you may tak' it back. But come in and hae yer four oors ! '

" Rob glowered hard at the beast, silently blasphemed, and thrust it back into the poke, and after a hearty meal started off again for Biggar, every now and then giving a sceptical keek into the poke to see that no change was taking place.

" Ritchie was waiting for him when he came to Candy-burn.

" ' Ye've been lang, Rob; and what for are ye carryin' the poke ower yer shouther ? '

" Rob was not sorry to get somebody to whom to tell his woeful tale.

" ' That's awfu', Rob, perfectly fearsome ! Ye maun step in an' hae a dram.   Oo maun tell Tibbie ! '

" As Rob flung down his poke, there was an unmistakable yowl.   Then he swallowed his dram, and began to tell his story.   Of course Ritchie quietly transferred the pig to the poke once more, and Rob started out again for Biggar feeling better after his dram, but fearing the reception he would get from his master.   On arriving he flung down his poke with a desperate air, and standing to attention, began declaring his sorrowful tale.

" ' A whaulp—an absolute whaulp, as ye may see wi' yer ain een,' he concluded.

" Opening the poke, he administered a vindictive kick to the beastie inside, and out came the pig of the morning.

" ' As fac's daith, Mr. Watson, it was a whaulp at Dowfintoun, and I lookit in noos and thans to see if it was turnin' out onything else, and it was a whaulp at Candyburn, and that Ritchie can aver an' sweer.'

" ' Nae doubt Ritchie kens a' aboot it,' said the wise old minister."

Chapter XXII

SCOUTS ON THE HILLS

" GIVE us grace and strength to forbear and to persevere. Give us courage and gaiety and the quiet mind. Spare to us our friends, soften to us our enemies. Bless us, if it may be, in all our innocent endeavours; if it may not, give us strength to encounter that which is to come, that we may be brave in peril, constant in tribulation, temperate in wrath, and in all changes of fortune, and down to the gates of death, loyal and loving to one another."

I think the man who wrote these words had the real Scout spirit—the spirit that would triumph over every difficulty, and win through in the hardest battles of life. He felt the thrill of life's grand adventure. You have only to read his books to know him—*Treasure Island, Kidnapped, Catriona, Travels with a Donkey in the Cevennes*.

Many of his poems and stories deal with the Pentland countryside. *The Body Snatcher*, for instance, brings in Penicuik, Fishers' Tryst, Auchendinny, and Glencorse. It is a tale of two Edinburgh medical students who, while engaged in digging in the old Glencorse Kirkyard, are greatly frightened by their lamp falling over the verge of the steep bank surrounding the graveyard, the

DOLPHINTON KIRK.

clanging sound of iron and broken glass echoing through the woods—then there is silence, and the sound of the marching rain ; and while on the way back to Edinburgh they become so terror-stricken as the swaying corpse, packed in a dripping sack and propped up between them in the gig, falls first on one of them and then on the other, that they think some change has taken place in it, and then upon deciding to have a look at it with the aid of the light of one of the gig lamps, they are so startled at what they see and recognize that with a yell they spring to the roadside, the lamp smashes to fragments, and the horse bolts and gallops into the city with its tell-tale load.

In *St. Ives* we have Monsieur de Saint Ives escaping from Edinburgh Castle down the rocks and fleeing to the cottage at Swanston, and fearing spring-guns and man-traps he finds refuge in the henhouse with its six sitting hens, and sleeps for sixteen hours. Staying with the Swanston shepherd are two drovers—Sim and Candlish—who are to take the road for England at the skreigh o' day, and St. Ives accompanies them. And so with a drove of shaggy sheep St. Ives and the wild, unkempt drovers in coarse homespun, shepherd's tartan plaids, with great sticks, and snuff-begrimed noses, begin the climb up the green track to the top of Howden Glen. There Stevenson imagines that they meet Sir Walter Scott on a hill pony, who goes with them for a quarter of an hour, and asks Sim if this is an amateur drover they have with them, and later remarks that " the pleasure of this country is much in the legends, which grow as plentiful as blackberries."

In *Picturesque Notes* we have places well known to every Scout—the haunted Hunters' Tryst, Comiston,

Fairmilehead, Bowbridge, and Caerketton; while as we read *Weir of Hermiston* our thoughts are passing over the moors and streams between Glencorse and the Lang Whang, the Cairn Hills, and the Cauldstaneslap. And Stevenson knew the grey memorial stones on Turnhouse and above Dunsyre, for he wrote of the " graves of the martyrs," and of the " standing stones on the vacant wine-red moor." But it is of his story in *Memories and Protraits* about the Swanston shepherd that I would speak—John Tod, " honest John," as he was known locally, who had a great influence on the life of young Stevenson. This is what Stevenson says about his friend :

" John was rough, he smelt of the windy brae; he had grit and dash, and that salt of the Old Adam that pleases men with any savage inheritance of blood, and he was a wayfarer besides, and took my gipsy fancy. . . .

" I owe my taste for that hillside business . . . to the art and interest of John Tod. He it was that made it live for me, as the artist can make all things live. It was through him the simple strategy of massing sheep upon a snowy evening, with its attendant scampering of earnest, shaggy aides-de-camp, was an affair that I never wearied of seeing, and that I never weary of recalling to mind; the shadow of the night darkening on the hills, inscrutable black bolts of snow shower moving here and there like night already come, huddles of yellow sheep and dartings of black dogs upon the snow, a bitter air that took you by the throat, unearthy harpings of the wind along the moors; and for centre-piece to all these features and influences, John, winding up the brae, keeping his captain's eye upon all sides, and breaking, ever and again, into a spasm of bellowing that seemed to make the evening bleaker. It is thus that I still see him in my mind's eye, perched on a hump of the declivity not far from Halkerside, his staff in airy flourish, his great voice taking hold upon the hills and echoing terror to the lowlands ; I, meanwhile, standing somewhat back, until the fit should be over, and, with a pinch of snuff, my friend relapse into his easy, even conversation."

The things he learned then he never forgot. That is what makes a Scout's life so vital and so interesting, because the things he learns in his youth he remembers for ever. What R. L. S. learned at Swanston was what he termed " that hillside business," the life and work of the shepherd, a great love for the countryside, for the hills—he calls them " Hills of Home "—and the heather and the clean, fresh wind a-blowing that made him leap up and say, " Life is good, God is good."

Tod took his business very seriously. At all times of the day and night he was up and along the hillsides, with his dogs and sheep. He was accustomed to the open spaces, to far horizons, to great silences. His dogs understood him, and when they received the orders which Tod roared out to them at the pitch of his voice, lo ! the hillside became a scene of intense interest, as the dogs carried out their master's commands and the sheep were gathered to the desired quarter. Tod could defy all weathers and brave the wildest winter's blast to shepherd his sheep. He knew the drove roads over the hills and over the Borders into England, by which he drove the sheep to the markets, and he knew also all about the dangers and adventures of the wild life of the drovers.

Now what did young Stevenson think of the shepherd?

At first he was afraid of him, for often he heard him bellow out his commands to the dogs in a voice like thunder, but he was a kindly man with a big, warm, generous heart, and he became a hero to Stevenson. Stevenson as a boy was quiet and thoughtful, always on the look-out for adventure, and he was always writing things down in a book, because he wanted to learn to write, and so Tod became a teacher to him. When Tod went his round on the hills, Stevenson went with him, and he learned the rich Scots dialect and all about " that hillside business." Tod used to say, " He's an' awfu' laddie for speirin' questions about a' thing, an' whenever you turn your back, awa' he gangs an' writes it a' doon."

Many wonderful talks they had together, and often at night when the winter storm roared along the hills and lashed them with rain or snow, Stevenson would pull aside his window blind and wonder if his friend, the shepherd, was out in it and caring for his sheep. This great love for the hills, for friends and animals, Stevenson learned when he was a boy. Often he wandered away alone, and sat down upon the hillside amid the great silence of the hills, and let it sink into his soul ; then he would listen for sounds, and jot them down in his book—the bleat of sheep and lambs, the trilling of curlews, the calling of gulls, and the whistling of plovers that warned the hares when danger was near and sent the rabbits scuttling headlong into their burrows. There was the challenging call of the red grouse—the king of the heather—the whir and croak of blackcock, and the golden plover's cry " Three-three " ; from the tree-tops came the stirring shouts of blackbirds and storm-cocks ; from the lush meadow grass the plaining of the corncrake

JOHN TOD, THE SWANSTON SHEPHERD.

and the whisper of the wind ; and the faint undertone of a hill burn chattering its way down over the hillside. There was the friendly smoke rising from the cottage chimneys ; upon the still air rose the sound of children's voices, the farm-dog's bark ; there was Ritchie, the ploughman, returning with his horses ; and in the far distance he would hear a farm cart rocking and jolting upon a hill road coming home for the night.

Who does not know all these sights and sounds ? We can never forget them. Stevenson never could. The Pentland Hills were graven on his heart, and John Tod, the Swanston shepherd, helped to grave them there, and among the last lines Stevenson wrote from Samoa in the South Seas were those of the " Hills of Home " :

> Blows the wind to-day, and the sun and rain are flying ;
> Blows the wind on the moors to-day . . .
> Where the whaups are crying,
> My heart remembers how ! "

Does not this appeal to every Scout ?

Who does not know the joy of a day upon the Pentland Hills and the tramp over the moors, the interest of every hill burn, the appetite, the meal, the camp, and the camp-fire, and, best of all, that quiet talk just before we go to rest, about the day's failures and successes, to-morrow's programme, thanks for the joys and gladness of the day, and of the Great Unseen Captain who guides the life of every Scout ?

R. L. S. had the Scout spirit ; his life was full of adventure ; he faced life bravely with his head up to the sun and the wind and the rain, and he had courage. What is courage ? Is it just—not being afraid ? No, it is sticking it when you *are* afraid ; *that* is courage.

To some he is a hero, because of his courageous chivalry, because of his love of the best in life.   He knew the spell of the road, and what it meant to sleep under the stars " at God's green caravanserai."

" Give to me the life I love,
    Let the lave go by me,
Give the jolly heaven above,
    And the by-way nigh me.

Bed in the bush with stars to see,
    Bread I dip in the river—
There's the life for a man like me,
    There's the life for ever."

He could light a fire and cook an evening meal, and use the carpenter's tools, but his best tool was his pen. He was loyal to God and to his friends, a cheery companion, and every one who reads his works will find him daily doing his " good turn."

Chapter XXIII

PENTLAND INFLUENCES ON R. L. S.*

IN reading the letters of Stevenson, those dated from Swanston are found to possess a distinction that causes us to pause and consider. We are not surprised that most of them are addressed to Mrs. Sitwell, to whom he unbosomed his inmost thoughts and feelings. Stevenson early heard and felt the Call of the Hills, and from that time, when he was seventeen years of age, until the day of his death he was their captive and they were his attendant spirits, causing him to search deeply within himself. The first beginnings of his love of Nature and of his philosophy of life had their birth there in the turbulent, impressionable days of youth.

The contemplation of the hills in quietness and in confidence gives strength, contentment, and peace. Wonder, awe, and reverence awake in the Hillman. They stir within him that strange product of intellect and emotion which we call imagination ; they bring gifts of vision and of faith ; they help to shape a man's philosophy of life ; they reveal its eternal purpose, and they formulate for him an ideal. Were these results conspicuously evident in the character of Stevenson, and can their source and their permanence in him be

* Paper read to the R. L. Stevenson Club in Stevenson's home, Howard Place, Edinburgh, October 10, 1929.

linked to the Pentlands which he heard calling to him all life long ?

The letters written at Swanston give us light. There a love of Nature was born in him ; the open air and sky, the far distances, and the hills, clear cut against the blue, made their appeal to him ; riotous bird-song and the sounds of farm and village were fresh revelations ; he discovered a new race in the Swanston country folks, and studied their Lowden characteristics. All that he ever knew of what he calls " that hillside business " he learned from Tod, the shepherd, as well as a new Scots vocabulary, and the meaning of service. Of Ritchie, the ploughman ; of Young, the gardener, and a host of others he learns and writes, and so becomes intensely interested—in himself.

The joy of open air exercise he frequently refers to. He revelled in the freedom of exploring these hills long before he walked the Chilterns, the Lake District, Galloway, and the Cevennes. He learned the secret of wooing Nature alone, with the mind open to impressions, and the thoughts taking colour from what is seen. He becomes a pipe for any wind to play upon ; he becomes strong and quiet like the hills ; and at the end of the day's walk he experiences what he calls " a peace that passes comprehension." Contentment and peace, but also revolt, divine discontent, and the adventurer's urge—all were his, so he will tell you when his heart glows warm. A rare combination of love of the open air as well as of the study, and that passion of heart to communicate what he has called " the incommunicable thrill of things," are part of the attraction of Stevenson to young folks to-day, and first became evident in him as effects of the Swanston residence.

ON LYNE WATER.

SCOUT CAMP.

The magic casements through which he looked at Swanston brought new revelations to him.   He awakens early one Sunday morning—first, a cock crew loudly and beautifully and often ; then followed a long interval of silence and darkness ; the grey morning began to get into his room, and then from the other side of the garden a blackbird executed one long flourish, and in a moment, as if a spring had been touched or a sluice gate opened, the whole garden just brimmed and ran over with bird songs.   And so he writes of the first bird chirp at the break of day :

> " In the belovèd hour that ushers day,
> In the pure dew, under the breaking grey,
> One bird, ere yet the woodland quires awake,
> With brief réveillé summons all the brake ;
> ' Chirp, chirp,' it goes ; nor waits an answer long ;
> And that small signal fills the grove with song."

He tells us how a hawk was disturbing the birds in the garden, and the whole place thrilled with little notes of warning and terror.   "I did not know before," he writes, " that the voice of birds could be so tragically expressive—they almost frightened me."

There are many illustrations of the delicacy of his feeling in the presence of Nature.   When he climbs to the top of Allermuir, and sees the face of Carnethy looking at him over the shoulder of Castlelaw, a sense of fear takes hold upon him.   He writes, " I never before to-day fully realized the haunting of such a gigantic face as it peers over into a valley and seems to command all corners."

When great beauty rose before his eyes, as in Silverado and in Samoa, he writes quietly about it, as one who felt delicately the impression of Nature, and was awed by the loveliness of what he saw and felt. The wonder born of the Pentlands was a preparation for the literary artist's appreciation of the sublime beauties of other lands.

In the Swanston days, and later, he loved to enter into the solitude of the hills alone—he longed for some of the peace of it in his own soul ; but bachelors might note that this disposition did not continue indefinitely ! Writing one of his intimate letters to Baxter in 1881, he said, " I don't care so much for solitude as I used to : result, I suppose, of marriage ! "

His wanderings among the hills brought him times of clear mental vision (*Virginibus Puerisque*), and from the awakened intellect and the aroused emotion there came that high gift of imagination that sent him in quest of a real philosophy of life. And this clear vision brought him faith. At least it sent him searching and seeking and questioning in his own soul concerning the meaning of experience in spiritual things. He saw God in Nature and in his own life experience. His conclusion was, " There is a manifest God for those who care to look for Him." His times of vision are associated with the country. He saw God there, and so the Pentlands were partly responsible for the early shaping of his stirring gospel of health and happiness amid the gloom of his times.

In his philosophy of life we still see him clinging to the hills. " Why this unceasing struggle ? " he says, ceaselessly marching, grudging yourself time for rest, indefatigable adventurous pioneers. . . . Soon, soon, it seems to you, you must come forth on some conspicuous hilltop, and but a little way farther against the setting

sun descry the spires of El Dorado." What is the use
of it, he asks; is there a goal at all? " Little do ye
know your own blessedness—for to travel hopefully is
better than to arrive, and the true success is to labour."
There is his philosophy, and you notice that the hilltop
is in it.

The Swanston letters form a picture of his changing
moods and of the " malady of twenty-three." He
becomes cynical, spiteful, moody, joyful, by turns: " I
am very jolly, having finished the writing of "Victor
Hugo." I have been reading Roman law and Calvin.
. . . I have had a long talk with the shepherd about
foreign lands, and sheep. . . ." He found life very
difficult to understand just then. He was not quite
sure. A few years later he was writing in more certain
terms of the " Unknown Steersman."

Here we have him then, writing from Swanston at
the age of twenty-three to twenty-five—years of crisis
and change—of the beauty of Nature, of peace, happiness, the responsibilities of life, death, immortality, of
being content and brave, looking eagerly for passages
of happiness by the wayside to be afterwards savoured
under the tongue.

At the end of a glorious June day in '75 he writes in
meditative mood—he is only twenty-five: " How the
years slip away, Colvin, and we walk little cycles, and
turn in little abortive spirals, and come out again, hot
and weary, to find the same view before us, the same
hill barring the road. . . . I feel quite happy, but
curiously inert and passive, something for the winds
to blow over and the sun to glimpse on and off again,
as it might be a tree or a gravestone. . . . The days
chase each other like sun patches, and the nights like

cloud shadows on a windy day ; content to see them go and no wise reluctant for the cool evening, with its *dew and stars* and *fading strain of magic red*. And I ask myself why I ever leave this humour ? What I have gained ? And the wind blows in the trees with a sustained ' pish,' and the birds answer me in a long derisive whistle."

How well we know the mood, how splendidly it is described ! These are the letters of a young man with personality, however unformed his faith.

There were also times when he was very happy at Swanston, even when indoors with Horace and Montaigne. " You may remember," he writes in *Virginibus*, " how Burns, numbering past pleasures, dwells upon the hours when he had been ' happy thinking.' Nowadays we are all so busy . . . that we can find no time for pleasure trips into the Land of Thought and among the Hills of Vanity. We are in such haste to be doing, to be writing, to be gathering gear, to make our voice audible for a moment in the derisive silence of Eternity, that we forget that one thing, of which these are but the parts, namely, to live."

Looking back on life, he describes the chase of the ideal ; the hills and streams are in it too :

> " Still
> Somewhere on the sunny hill
> Or along the winding stream
> Through the willows flits a dream,
> Flits but shows a smiling face,
> Flies but with so quaint a grace
> None can choose to stay at home,
> All must follow, all must roam—
> This is unborn beauty."

There is more significance in the Pentland influence than has ever been told. None other of his many habitations set its seal upon Stevenson's heart as the Pentlands did. "My imagination continually inhabits that cold old huddle of grey hills," he writes to J. M. Barrie from the sunny South. And why? Because in these momentous days of early manhood he heard the insistent call for vigour and decision, and it was there that he answered it, amid the quiet of rural Swanston. "Happiness came to him chiefly in the country," says Mr. Graham Balfour. How often he retired to the thought and atmosphere of the Hills of Home for an understanding of life. And that heart cry—as in imagination he hears the shrill echo of the pee-wees calling! Give me nothing more. I see it all—the Hills of Home—what memories!

Memories of walks and talks along the foothills with his father, earnest conversations with his mother and with Cummy, heart-aching letters to Mrs. Sitwell, Colvin, and others; the acceptance and rejection of magazine articles, advice from Leslie Stephen; reading law; journeys to and from the city; memories of that never-to-be-forgotten idyll when he saw the little girl at the cottage door at Fairmilehead embrace her dog, and exclaim, "I love ye, Jock," and how it made him happy all the day. Memories of Saturday afternoons with Inglis searching for uncommon wild-flowers and birds' eggs, jolly week-ends with Ferrier, Simpson, and Baxter; drives with the convalescing Henley; that moonlight night in May—after the Sunday at Glencorse Kirk with his father—when he walked out to Swanston, accompanied as far as Fairmilehead by his cousin Bob, with whom he had been dining, with its hilarious and jovial mirth, its " profuse bursts of unpremeditated song," that " night worth gold untold " ; and his arrival home at Swanston after the yachting tour in the West Highlands, having " left his pipe on board the yacht, his umbrella in the dog-cart, and his portmanteau by the way," minus his luggage, and in a borrowed hat and borrowed coat—what memories !

And all the anticipated joy of writing about the jolly old exciseman at Bowbridge Distillery, and his " over the hills and far away " ; and the revels of the Six Foot Club at Hunters' Tryst, after the forty miles' walk on the Saturday—" Ye Gods, didn't I make them sit up, or rather lie down, under the table and in the barn," we can imagine him saying, " their red faces mixed in the straw like plums in a cake," and Forbes covered with candle-creish like a man in a snowstorm, and how I sent them all to Colinton Kirk in the morning, with their tails between their legs and their tongues hanging out ! And then the fun of locking up St. Ives in the outhouse with six sitting hens, and letting him sleep for sixteen hours before he joined the drovers at the Howden Hass, and the meeting with old Sir Walter with his fishing rod at the head of the glen ; and " ha ! ha ! ha ! he gave me a cigar ! "

And how Stevenson must be laughing now, if he hears the busmen's tales at the old Glencorse Kirk. " There is where Maister Stevenson wrote all his works," says one, pointing to the old graveyard. " Louis Stevenson was aye quarrelling wi' the meenister o' that kirk," says another.

In " Evensong " we see his full surrender, and the hills and the woods and the breeze and the cottage are in it too :

" The breeze from the embalmèd land
　Blows sudden toward the shore,
　And clasps my cottage door.
　I hear the signal, Lord—I understand.
　The night at Thy command
　Comes. I will eat and sleep and will not question
　　more."

All through life he gazed upon the hilltops because
he had lived at Swanston, and at the end he was buried
on a hilltop—" the hunter home from the hill "—the
hunter's trysting-place at Swanston linked by a thousand
memories with the hunter's home in sunny Samoa.

Religion was a vital thing to Stevenson, and it too
is bound up with the Pentland days. His first literary
effort was an essay on Moses, then came a history of
Joseph, and his first published pamphlet of twenty-two
pages was *The Pentland Rising*, at the age of sixteen.
We remember Cummy's influence. At the age of forty-
one, from Vailima, he gives his opinions on the Covenanters : " I am a child of the Covenanters, whom I
do not love, but they are mine after all, my father's
and my mother's—and they had their merits too, and
their ugly beauties and grotesque heroisms that I love
them for, the while I laugh at them."

He wrote from America to Crockett that he was not
a kirkgoer, and gave his reasons, among them the
sermon. As a young man Stevenson was a kirkgoer,
but he says little about the sermons. We know that
instead of listening to Mr. Bisset of Ratho preaching in
Old Greyfriars, he was copying out a very beautifully
expressed prayer which he had found in the pew in a
volume of Family Prayers. On this subject of preaching,
Stevenson once made a very incisive remark, as applic-

able to-day as then : " What is the use," he asked, " of
a man preaching a sermon, however polished, however concise, and convincing in itself, unless it is de-
livered in such a spirit as to move those who hear it ?
The wisest words and the best sentiments coming from
a wooden image are lost for ever, and no one benefits."

But what he learned in Glencorse Kirk we shall never
know.　Scotsmen have the habit of concealing the deep
things of their belief, and sacred feelings seldom find
expression.　Stevenson was no exception.　That his
attendance at Glencorse Kirk meant much to him is
manifest in these letters.　In this respect also the
Pentland influence was real and lasting.

The period between Stevenson's youth and manhood
was a tremendously vital time in his life, and it is the
fact that the Call of the Pentlands came to him at that
time that makes the Swanston period stand out so clearly,
dominating his future life and thought ; a time when he
received many a shock, in which he did some very hard
thinking alone ; there was no counsellor along these
lines, no one like-minded to help.　I believe that Swanston and the Pentlands saved him—the voice of the
" Unknown Steersman " was in the Call of the Hills.
Here was his " desert," in which in quietness he thought
out what he was to do with life as he saw it, and to form
his philosophy ; and then he gripped hard at the things
that remained, and frequently changed his opinions.
Life held many ugly features, but as Mr. G. K. Chesterton remarks in his critical study—the most masterly
that has yet appeared — Stevenson believed in a
" potential poetry of life, and he was bewildered by
its apparently impossible position in the world of real
living."　He declined to worship comfort and respecta-

"HILLS OF HOME."

bility as substitutes for active and courageous well-doing. He was no sentimentalist. He was profoundly sincere. "I do not think," says Chesterton, "that time of transition from the Child's Garden of Verses to the Man's Garden of Vows went right with Stevenson." I think it would have gone much worse if there had been no Swanston and no Pentland Hills. They were his study after the playroom, and more attention has been paid to the playroom than to the study—into which, we shall do well to mark, he carried his pictures of pirates and red gold and bright blue seas, and looked at them anew with the literary student's eye. True, it was then that he ate the apple of knowledge, like most of us, only in his case "it was a crab apple." But he was different from most, and he rose on stepping-stones to mountain heights. "I to the hills will lift mine eyes," he quoted, and then added, "There are days in a life when thus to climb out of the lowlands seems like scaling heaven."

It may have been a puritanic and pessimistic age. Well, Stevenson rebelled against it, he wanted things stated positively, clear cut, sharply outlined, bright, colourful—like Caerketton against the skyline, all purple in the evening light and pearly as at dawn.

Stevenson never forgot childhood; his letters consistently express his love for children, and the child in him never grew up. As he sat upon the Swanston hillside meditating, I am sure he heard the sound of children's voices rising upon the still air. "He seemed to skip upon the hills of life," says Mr. Gosse, referring to his gaiety; "a childlike mirth leaped and danced in him."

He loved simplicity and colour—Alan Breck Stewart

must wear a bright blue French coat with bright silver buttons, Glenure must have red hair, and his servant must be laden with lemons—a bright yellow. It's all bound up in the Pentland associations of Colinton, Swanston, and Glencorse, and " The Lowden Sabbath Morn."

" The key to his career was early put into his hands ; it is well symbolized by the paint brush dipped in purple and Prussian blue with which he started to colour the stiff caricatures upon the cardboard of Skelt. He also painted in water colours : for of such is the Kingdom of Heaven "—so Chesterton.

But his Garden of Gethsemane also was at Swanston —whether he was there in person, or in Edinburgh, London, or Paris. It was there he fought it out amid the silence of the hills. There is Stevenson's shrine, where we too may make pilgrimage, and listen to the voices in the silence, to the pee-wees crying, and to the sound of children's voices upon the still air. Refreshed, we shall return to refashion our own lives, bright, joyful, invigorated, and with a surging desire for service, indifferent to conventionalities and the judgment of blind self-seekers.

The Call of the Pentlands—we have seen some of its effects. " When you climb to Halkerside and sprinkle the well water on the turf, sain it wi' a bit prayer ; and tell the pee-wees I mind their forebears well. My heart is sometimes heavy and sometimes glad to mind it all." His heart was in the hills, the winds austere and pure, the springtime odours of the moorlands, the hills of sheep, the wild-birds crying and screaming—his heart, with its infectious joy in active living ; here is the faith that shines through personality :

> " O to be up and doing, O
> Unfearing and unshamed to go
> In all the uproar and the press
> About my human business ! "

And what entered into the soul of Stevenson in these Swanston days, found in due season expression in his works, for he not only heard but answered, the Call of the Pentlands.

THE END

PRINTED IN GREAT BRITAIN AT
THE PRESS OF THE PUBLISHERS